The
Australian Shepherd
Champion of Versatility

Liz Palika

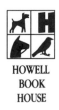

HOWELL
BOOK
HOUSE

Howell Book House
A Simon & Schuster Macmillan Company
1633 Broadway
New York, NY 10019

MACMILLAN is a registered trademark of Macmillan, Inc.

Library of Congress Cataloging-in-Publication Data

Palika, Liz, 1954-
    The Australian shepherd : champion of versatility / Liz
  Palika.
        p. cm.
    Includes index.
    ISBN 0-87605-039-9
    1. Australian shepherd dog. I. Title
SF429.A79P35 1995
636.7'37--dc20   95-3753
                                                                  CIP

Book & Jacket Design:
  Catherine Swain
  Adine Maron Design
  Chroma Litho

Illustrations:
  Gail Trower

Manufactured in United States of America
10   9   8   7   6   5   4

This book is dedicated to Beth Donnelly, and Ralph and Eileen Swingle, who, when I was searching for the "perfect" breed, shared their Aussies with me and their enthusiasm for the breed.

This book is also dedicated to Marie Dailey. My words cannot express the joy your dogs have given me. Thank you for selling me two of the most wonderful dogs in the world.

Finally, I would like to offer my heartfelt appreciation to Catherine Swain for her generous assistance above and beyond the call of duty. Without her dedication and love for Aussies, this book would not have been completed.

Table of Contents

CHAPTER 1

The Australian Shepherd

*"The Australian Shepherd seems very much American,
an amalgamation of traits from across the seas—intelligence, loyalty
and unique beauty combined with physical agility for ease in
doing the job they enjoy so much."*

RACHEL PAGE ELLIOT,
AUSTRALIAN SHEPHERD CLUB OF AMERICA YEARBOOK, 1957–1977.

"I don't care if my dogs are pretty," the rancher said as his work-callused hand rested on the head of a blue merle Australian Shepherd, "I need a dog that has the instincts to work stock. He needs to be gentle with the lambs and rough with the steers. He needs to think for himself but still take direction."

Keith Talbert works a ranch that his great-grandfather originally homesteaded. He and his wife raise working Australian Shepherds, sheep, dairy cows and horses, as well as three young sons.

"I need a dog that will be good with my boys, yet have the stamina to work with me all day and I'm out here from sunup to sunset. He's got to be healthy—I can't be babying a dog, you know."

Keith's expression contradicted the toughness of his words but his next comment reflected the opinion of most Australian Shepherd breeders and fanciers, "I want a sound mind in a sound body."

The Australian Shepherd today is an attractive dog as well as a sound, healthy dog. Known for its bobbed tail and beautiful merle coloring, the Aussie is medium-sized, eighteen to twenty-three inches tall at the shoulder, averaging between forty-five and sixty pounds, with the bitches smaller than the dogs. Coat colors include black, red (liver), blue merle (black, gray and silver) and red merle (brown, red, rust and sorrel) any of which can be offset by copper and white trim.

With its smoothly flowing trot and natural athletic ability, as well as its strong guardian and herding instincts, the Aussie has excelled as a working stockdog. Known for its ability to work a variety of livestock, from ducks, sheep and cattle, to geese, goats and pigs, the Aussie is also a versatile stockdog. Although not normally recommended because of the danger to the dog, Aussies have even worked horses and American bison.

The Aussie is more than just a stockdog; it is also very much a companion dog. An Aussie is happiest when doing something— anything—with its owner. No matter whether it is going for a walk, playing Frisbee, riding in the car, playing with the kids, running alongside a horse, or simply lying by its owner's feet as he or she reads, Australian Shepherds need to be with their people.

Australian Shepherds have strong guardian instincts which were origi- nally developed to guard livestock from predators or thieves, but are easily transferred to people. Because of these strong instincts, Aussies feel a need to be close to and protect their family and can be quite formidable protectors. Many Aussies have put themselves in danger to protect their owners from raging bulls, goats in rut and protective mother cows, as well as bears and other predators. Aussies haven't

Circa 1900, Wyoming.

Circa 1918, Wyoming.

hesitated to protect their owners from human predators, either. Muggers, purse snatchers and burglars have been sent on their way by protective Aussies.

Although protective of their own and reserved with strangers, Aussies make friends for life. Once an Australian Shepherd has decided that you are a friend, you will be remembered forever and greeted with smiles and a wagging rear end every time you meet. Because of this orientation to people, Australian Shepherds are not good backyard dogs, to be left outside and separated from people. An unhappy Aussie will become depressed, morose and will develop behavior problems: barking, digging, chewing or escaping from the yard.

One of the traits that appeals to many people is the Aussie's versatility. The breed's trainability is so important it is mentioned prominently in the breed standard. This trainability, coupled with its natural intelligence, allows Australian Shepherd owners to try new avenues for the breed to excel in, and excel it has. You can see Aussies competing in obedience, winning Frisbee-catching competitions, pulling carts and wagons, working as guide dogs for the blind and service dogs for the disabled. Aussies have competed in schutzhund alongside German Shepherds and Rottweilers, and have served admirably on search and rescue teams. An Aussie's capabilities are limited only by the imaginations of the people who own them.

Myths and Mysteries

Herding dogs were probably first used about 12,000 years ago, although some researchers say that it might have been as early as 25,000 years ago. Written records, of course, are not available, but cave drawings have shown men and dogs chasing after deer, elk and the ancestors of modern cattle. We do know that herding dogs developed in several different parts of the world, including different areas of Europe and the British Isles, Asia and the Americas.

The early history of the Australian Shepherd is unknown. Some breed historians feel that the breed is a mixture of herding breeds that came to America with early settlers from Europe. Other researchers are convinced that the breed originated in Europe, went to Australia and then came to California and North America during the Gold Rush. The myths that surround the origins of the breed are, to some people, one of the tantalizing aspects of the breed.

Circa 1910, South Dakota.

Early North America

Early American history is threaded with bits of information concerning sheep, shepherds and their herding dogs. Christopher Columbus, who made four trips to the New World (1492–1502) brought sheep with him to North America on at least two of these trips. The British explorers (early 1600s) did not bring sheep with them that we know of, but the settlers who followed did, and with these sheep came their dogs. The British herding dogs included Dorset Blue Shags, Smithfield Sheepdogs and Cumberland Sheepdogs. The Blue Shags and the Smithfield are related to the old Scottish Collie and the Cumberland is a Border Collie type dog.

The Spanish also figured prominently among immigrants who brought domestic animals to the New World. Merino sheep and their wonderful wool had ensured Spain a primary place in the world trade markets in the 1500 and 1600s and although Spain was famous for its cattle and horses, sheep were the mainstay of the economy. Therefore, when the Spanish immigrated to the Americas, both North and South, they brought their sheep with them. The Spanish explorers had sheep with them, too, and when exploring the west coast of the continent in the 1500s, even released sheep and goats on off-shore islands to survive, reproduce and be available as ready sources of meat. (Several populations still exist today off the coast of California.)

By the late 1600s and early 1700s, immigrants from several nations were flooding into North America, some bringing the tools of their trade while others just had the shirts on their backs. People who worked the land in their native countries knew the importance of livestock and those immigrants brought their livestock and dogs with them to the New World. Immigrants from Scotland brought the Scottish Collie (a Bearded Collie type dog) with them while immigrants from Wales brought along Welsh Grey Sheepdogs, also a Bearded Collie type breed. Irish immigrants brought the Glenwherry Collie to America, a Border Collie type dog and the French imported the Bouvier des Flandres. The Germans, who also brought Merino sheep to the New World, brought along their German Shepherds and the Hutespitz, a Spitz-type dog.

One of the more popular dogs imported was the English Shepherd. Called a farm

Circa 1917, Wyoming

collie in early America, the English Shepherd could herd livestock, protect the family against wild animals and warn off trespassers, too. The English Shepherd today looks much like an Australian Shepherd. There is no way to prove it, but many people feel that the English Shepherd is an ancestor to today's Australian Shepherd.

As immigrants and dogs came to America from all over Europe, crossing of the various breeds took place. Eventually, as the different regions were settled and communities were established, each area developed a particular type of herding dog suited to their particular needs. These dogs were called by a variety of names, including Spanish Shepherd, Bob-Tails, California Shepherds, Pastor Dogs, Blues and New Mexican Shepherds.

Stories abound as to how exactly, the breed came to be called the "Australian Shepherd." Notes in personal diaries, stories told to grandchildren, and old photographs show us that a dog similar to today's Aussie was very much a part of early North American, and especially Western, life. But where did it come from? It might be a cross-breeding of British-type herding dogs that served as farm dogs all over the country or it might have come from the Basque country of Europe by way of Australia. The breed might have descended from Basque sheepdogs or it might be a combination of all of the above.

Like many Americans, the Aussie is very much a part of the American melting pot. At different times during the breed's recent history, it has even been suggested that the breed's name should be changed from Australian Shepherd to American Shepherd. At some time in the future this may come about. Although the breed is and has been known for many years as the Australian Shepherd, it is very much an American breed.

Australia

In the 1700s, people were also attracted to Australia. The Germans, French, Irish and Welsh moved there, bringing their livestock and dogs. The German Coulie is a herding dog that looks very much like today's Aussie and might figure in the breed's heritage. The British came in great numbers, infusing Australia with their customs, language and, of course, their dogs.

As the popularity of sheep herding spread throughout Australia, herding dogs became a necessity. When Merino sheep were imported to Australia, Spanish and Basque shepherds came to care for them, bringing their Pyrenees Sheepdogs and Catalan Sheepdogs. As in North America, a lot of mixed breeding took place, some intentionally, some by accident.

The Basque Mystique

The Basque people live in, or are from, the western Pyrenees in France and Spain. An interesting fact about the Basque people is that their language has no known relationship to any other language in the world. Nor do the Basque people have any written language; history is passed on through stories and songs told to youngsters by the older generations.

The Basque people are credited with the development of some wonderful herding dogs, including, some experts say, the ancestors of the Australian Shepherd. Many Australian Shepherd historians believe that the modern Australian Shepherd is the descendant of Basque sheepdogs that went to Australia and then to North America, following the herds of sheep.

Family portrait, Custer County, Nebraska, circa 1887.

Russell S. Peer in 1922 with his Aussie puppy "Nancy" and his pig "Jim."

Dr. William Douglas, a historian at the University of Nevada, stated, "What the young Basque males brought to America was a rural upbringing that gave them some skill in caring for livestock, a propensity for hard work, and a willingness to undergo extreme hardship in order to get ahead. It was here, under the tutelage of an experienced herder, that the new arrival learned how to herd sheep."

The Basque people did have some nice herding dogs which were eagerly sought after by other shepherds and there were reports of dogs being imported from Spain in the 1800s. As with many of the herding dogs imported to Australia and North America, these dogs, which were similar in type to Bearded Collies or Briards, were often crossed with other herding dogs; breed integrity was not always important, a good working dog was.

However, one fact many historians either do not realize or have forgotten is that many of the Basque immigrants to both Australia and North America were not shepherds in their homeland. Some were, of course, but many of the Basque immigrants came to Australia and America for the same reasons that immigrants from other countries came: to make a living or a fortune, to have more personal freedom or to simply better themselves. When they found that the streets were not paved with gold, they learned many crafts, including how to be shepherds.

Old Blue Boy, 1946.

Jay Sisler, his Aussies and Greta the Greyhound.

Taming the West

The California Gold Rush brought a flood of people to California. Some sought to make their fortunes panning for gold while others made a fortune by selling equipment to the miners, often at an outrageous price. Food was at times in short supply, and flocks of sheep were brought in to feed and clothe the hordes.

The history of the West during the late 1800s is filled with tall tales and the Australian Shepherd's history during that time period is the same. Putting the romance of the West aside, most of the people who moved westward in the 1800s were trying to make a new life, trying to homestead land where they could raise their family. Other than a few personal diaries, written records from the early years are almost nonexistent; however, a few photographs remain that show dogs resembling Australian Shepherds posed with Western homesteaders and families. A loyal, intelligent, trainable herding and working dog was needed and the Australian Shepherd, as the breed type was coming into being, fit right in.

The Aussie in the 1900s

JAY SISLER

Jay Sisler, a talented dog trainer from Idaho, did more to promote the Australian Shepherd than anyone else in the breed's history. Sisler spent twenty years of his life traveling with his "Blue dogs," giving shows at rodeos and amazing people with the tricks that his wonderfully trained dogs would do.

Sisler had Aussies before the breed was well known as the Australian Shepherd, acquiring Keno his first "Blue dog," as he called them, in 1939, the dog he called his first "Good dog". His foundation bitch, Blue Star, was bought at a livestock auction. Her pedigree is unknown, but, when bred with Keno, she produced two dogs Shorty and Stub—that went on to be two of Sisler's most impressive rodeo trick dogs.

Sisler and his dogs performed in the 1950s and 1960s. Crowds everywhere agreed that his dogs were absolutely amazing. They would stand on their heads, balance on bars, jump rope, climb ladders and much, much more. Their acts greatly increased interest in the breed, especially in the Northwestern United States and Canada.

Stub, Shorty and Jay Sisler jump rope at the National Western Stockdog Show, Denver 1954.

Jay Sisler's dogs Shorty and Stub "pulling the pants off" Slim Pickens in a scene from the movie Cowdog.

the star of Sisler's act for a number of years and a Disney movie, *Cowdog* was based on his life and talents. Today his lines show up in many modern pedigrees. Shorty was the sire of Sisler's Joker, whose granddaughter, Taylor's Buena, became an important breed foundation bitch, producing Hartnagle's Hud and Homer's Jill, that produced Las Rocasa Shiloh. Shorty's most important son was probably Wood's Jay, (1950–1964) who became a foundation sire himself and from whom descended a multitude of wonderful dogs, including Wood's Stubby (Wood's Jay X Wood's Slate) and Nettesheim's Twinkle (Wood's Jay X Nightingale's Tammy), from whom descended Heard's Cactus of Flintridge, Saga of Flintridge and Heard's Savor.

Sisler was not a breeder as many people define it; he did not breed a great number of litters. However, he and his brother Gene did breed a little and the resulting dogs contributed to many of the modern Aussie lines, passing on intelligence, trainability and a desire to work.

Sisler's Shorty (1948–1959) sired many of the breed's most important foundation stock. He was a good looking, great working blue merle with lots of personality. He was

"Mac," a great grandson of Sisler's Shorty, brings Maggie Sisler her hat.

Ch. Las Rocosa Shiloh, ASCA Hall of Fame Sire.

Hartnagle's Hud, ASCA Honor Roll Sire.

Fletcher Wood, the ringmaster at the National Western Livestock Show near Denver, bought Wood's Jay (Sisler's Shorty X Sisler's Trixie) from Jay Sisler. He also bought a dog named Blue from Juanita Ely of Littleton, Colorado, who had started her line of dogs in the 1950s after acquiring Ely's Blue from Gene Sisler.

FLINTRIDGE

Noel Heard acquired a red herding dog named Old Jim in 1928. Old Jim was said to be an Australian Shepherd, out of a blue merle bitch. After growing up with Old Jim, Noel's son, Weldon Heard, a veterinarian schooled in genetics, later recommended a client to an Aussie breeder, Fletcher Wood, and through a convoluted chain of events, ended up with an Aussie bitch named Mistingo. Mistingo was bred to Harper's Old Smokey, one of the breed's foundation sires, producing two pups, one of which was

Heard's Blue Spice of Flintridge, that became Dr. Heard's foundation bitch. She was bred back to Old Smokey, producing Heard's Salt of Flintridge and Heard's Chili of Flintridge; both of whom produced a number of champions in the 1970s and are still seen on pedigrees today.

Two other important Flintridge dogs were Wildhagen's Dutchman of Flintridge (The Herdsman of Flintridge X Heards Savor of Flintridge), and Fieldmaster of Flintridge (The Herdsman of Flintridge X Heards Savor of Flintridge). Both dogs were successful in shows and as sires, increasing the popularity and interest of the Flintridge line.

Dr. Heard's biggest contribution to the breed was his practice of strong linebreeding with good quality dogs, defining quality as a combination of conformation, working ability and intelligence. He selectively bred bitches in his line back to proven Flintridge sires. This standarized his line, creating dogs of close

Flintridge foundation sires, Cactus of Flintridge, The Herdsman of Flintridge and Salt of Flintridge.

type and quality. When these dogs were then introduced into other bloodlines, with their progeny bred back to Flintridge, the related lines became stronger in type.

STEVE MANSKER

Steve Mansker saw Jay Sisler and his dogs at numerous rodeos in the late 1940s and decided that he wanted one of those dogs. He bought Sisler's Freckles in 1956. Freckles was bred to Green's Kim, a large blue merle that was an outstanding cowdog. That breeding produced Mansker's Anna Lee.

A granddaughter of Freckles Duchess, was a tremendous working dog, and when bred with Smokey—also a great cowdog— Duchess produced Mansker's Turk. Turk was a superb working dog and became a great sire

producing sound, good-looking working dogs. Taylor's Rusty (Mansker's Turk X Sisler's Freckles) and Taylor's Whiskey (Mansker's Turk X Mansker's Anna Lee) became influential sires in their own right.

Mansker used judicious linebreeding to keep the great working instinct that he had in his early dogs. These dogs went on to establish the foundation of many of today's important working kennels, including Hartnagle's Las Rocosa, Joe Taylor's Australian Shepherds, some of the Slash V Aussies and some of the Casa de Carrillo dogs.

ASCA

The Australian Shepherd Club of America (ASCA) was incorporated in 1957 as the parent organization for Australian Shepherds, although, a number of other associations registered or served the Aussie, too. The International Australian Shepherd Association (IASA), formed in 1966 and

Ch. Slash V Rocky Top, pictured with Scott Martin, 1972.

headquartered in California, offered show and obedience programs and in the early 1970s had a breed registry. The Mountains and Plains Blue Australian Shepherd Club was formed in Colorado in the late 1950s. This club's first President was long-time Aussie breeder Juanita Ely.

Between 1960 and 1967 ASCA, missing strong leadership, became dormant. As a result, IASA was formed. IASA played an important role in the development of the breed and sparked ASCA into action; by 1970, ASCA had created a registry and a show program and became the first rare breed club to offer conformation championships based upon the AKC model.

By 1980, ASCA had absorbed the IASA registrations. By merging the registry, the Australian Shepherd Club of America became the single parent club to serve the breed. At this writing, ASCA presently has over 73,000 individual dogs registered and a membership of 4,800 people.

One of ASCA's important functions is to maintain a breed standard. The standard is a description of the "perfect" Australian Shepherd, itemizing appearance, structure, movement and temperament. The standard being used today by ASCA was written by a committee headed by Robert E. Kline, D.V.M., and was approved in January, 1977.

Above, Harper's Old Smokey (1957-1972), a foundation sire, made a significant contribution to the development of the Australian Shepherd.
Below, Hartnagle's Fritzie Taylor, ASCA Honor Roll Dam.

Ch. Wildhagen's Dutchman of Flintridge, pictured winning Best of Breed at the IASA National Specialty, 1970. "Dusty" was the first ASCA Conformation Champion of Record, Companion Dog and Companion Dog Excellent; an Honor Roll Sire and Best of Breed winner at the ASCA National Specialty, 1970.

ASCA's Stockdog Program, which was organized in 1974, was designed to preserve and promote the herding instincts of the Australian Shepherd and to encourage Aussie owners to become involved in this aspect of their dogs heritage by offering titles and awards.

ASCA is primarily a breed registry, but has placed much of its emphasis on maintaining the natural working ability of the breed and stressing its natural athletic abilities, its trainability and versatility. Recently, the organization has instituted a DNA genetic testing program to ensure the breed's continued purity.

ASCA offers Australian Shepherd owners a program to show their dogs in conformation where the dogs are judged against each other and the breed standard. Championships are awarded and the Top Ten Conformation dogs each year are eligible to compete in the Purina Invitational All Breed Dog Show and in the Tournament of Champions.

ASCA also offers owners a chance to show their dog in obedience competition, awarding several different titles, including Obedience Trial Champion. ASCA recognizes the top ten obedience dogs each year and Aussies qualifying within ASCA's program are eligible to compete in the Gaines/Cycle Obedience Championships held across the country each year.

Ch. Copper Canyon Caligari CD, Winners Dog and Best of Winners at the ASCA National Specialty, 1976; Winners Dog, Best of Winners and Best of Breed at the ASCA National Specialty, 1977. An ASCA Hall of Fame Sire, "Jimmie" was handled by Erin George.

Ch. Propwash St. Elmo's Fire pictured at eight weeks of age, later in life became an ASCA Hall of Fame Sire and Best of Breed winner at the USASA National Specialty, 1993.

Enter the American Kennel Club

When the Australian Shepherd Club of America was founded in 1957, in Arizona, its goal was to promote the Australian Shepherd with the idea of one day pursuing American Kennel Club (AKC) recognition. Many members protested such recognition, fearing that the breed would lose its working heritage. Recognition did not come about at that time, nor during other instances in the 1970s when the subject was brought up again by the International Australian Shepherd Association or by ASCA members.

According to Australian Shepherd Club of America Historian Phil Wildhagen, in 1975, ASCA had its first membership vote on AKC recognition and the outcome was affirmative. However, the Board of Directors was composed largely of stock-dog-oriented members who failed to act on the membership mandate,

and nothing was done. In 1985 another membership vote was taken and went down to defeat by a two to three margin.

On April 18, 1991 the Board of Directors of the American Kennel Club approved a new procedure for the application and approval of breeds eligible for the Miscellaneous Class and the first breed to test this procedure was the Australian Shepherd. This recognition was the work of a small group of Australian Shepherd owners who had formed the United States Australian Shepherd Association (USASA) for the purpose of pursuing AKC recognition.

The long-time parent club, the Australian Shepherd Club of America (ASCA) was unaware of the plans until the official press release. ASCA members and supporters were concerned that AKC recognition would undermine decades of breeding, registries and championships and that this wonderful breed would become another pretty show dog with little or no working instinct.

Ch. Propwash St. Elmo's Fire as an adult.

USASA and AKC members and supporters stressed that AKC recognition simply offered Aussie owners another venue for competition, much like United Kennel Club and States Kennel Club recognition, and that it would in no way harm the breed. It did not take long for the Australian Shepherd to be promoted from the Miscellaneous Class to the Herding Group, with full competition privileges; in fact, the first Aussie competed in the prestigious Westminster Kennel Club Show, in the Herding Group, in 1993.

The AKC offers a conformation show program where dogs can compete for breed championships and then move onto the interbreed competition culminating in Best in Show at all breed shows. The AKC also offers obedience competition, tracking, agility and herding events, all available to the Aussie. Many Aussies are now registered with both the AKC and ASCA, as well as other registries, including the States Kennel Club, United Kennel Club and the Canadian Kennel Club, to name just a few. These talented dogs are competing, winning and earning show, obedience and performance titles in many different arenas.

Ch. Bayshore's Flapjack winning Best of Breed at the Westminster Kennel Club Dog Show, 1994.

Ch. Hemi's Regal Request CD STDs OTDd

"Hymie"

OWNERS: GARY AND MARY HAWLEY
BREEDER: HAZEL SNOW, HAZELWOOD AUSSIES

Hymie came into this world on August 26, 1972; a brilliant blue merle with white trim. He was a smart little pup and as a result, pretty much got his way with everything. He was a natural show off, which helped in the conformation ring. Hymie is an ASCA Hall of Fame sire, one of only two in the state of Arizona, and was the Windsor Aussies foundation sire.

Hymie was a varmint hunter, an outstanding fly-ball dog and loved scent hurdle races. His scent hurdle team, "The Wild Bunch" was comprised of all Windsor Aussies and was undefeated.

Mary Hawley said, "We have many memories of Hymie, some of which we consistently see in the many pictures and artwork of him. He is one of the Aussies on the ASCA display board, and there is a pen and ink drawing of him in the 1994 Australian Shepherd Annual by noted artist Ingrid Johnson. An illustration of Hymie was used for the Arizona Australian Shepherd Club logo as a dedication to his importance, as all of the founding members had Hymie kids."

CHAPTER 2

Is an Aussie the Right Dog for You?

BEFORE YOU RUSH out and get an Australian Shepherd, or any dog for that matter, there are some questions you need to ask yourself. First of all, do you really need a dog? The decision to add a dog to your family is not a decision to be taken lightly. A dog requires a commitment on your part to love and care for this animal for the next fourteen to sixteen years. You will need to make sure you have the time, energy, affection, ability and finances to care for its every need. Nor should an Aussie, or any dog, be purchased as a playtoy for a child. Very few children are responsible enough to care for a dog without adult supervision.

Abandoning a half-grown or adult Aussie at the local animal shelter because you are too busy or are moving is irresponsible, as is allowing your child to neglect the dog. Before getting an Aussie, think through this decision carefully, because once you decide to get a dog, it is, or should be, a lifetime commitment.

Is your personality suited to an Aussie? Australian Shepherds are very devoted to their people and when not working or exercising, should be inside with their owners. This means you will have a fuzzy shadow everywhere you go. Once you get used to it, this can be very enjoyable; you will have

Exercise is essential for the health of your Aussie.

something to do on its own. That something might be digging up the backyard, herding the family cats or barking at the neighbors—negative problems that might have been prevented through time spent with the dog and training.

All Aussies require training, so if you do not have the patience, compassion and perseverance to train a dog, do not get an Aussie. As with many intelligent working or herding breed dogs, Aussies are smart enough to get into trouble if they are not taught the household rules. Training also keeps the dog's

someone to talk to that listens to every word you say, a soft head to pat and ear to scratch and a warm fuzzy body to hug whenever you want. It can have a downside: you will have company when you go to the bathroom, you will have to watch for paws when you push back your chair and you will trip on a dog every time you turn around. So, if having a second shadow bothers you, do not get an Aussie.

Because of its loyalty, devotion and strong desire to please, the Australian Shepherd can be a great companion. However, because of its strong working instincts, it can also make a poor pet. How can a dog be both a great companion and a poor pet? Easy. Every Aussie needs a job to do, a sense of being needed. If an Aussie does not have that need satisfied, does not have a means of using up excess energy and an activity to keep its mind occupied, it will find

mind busy, helping to alleviate boredom. Bored Aussies can be very imaginative: opening cupboard doors, turning doorknobs or climbing up onto counters. Training also helps establish the dog's position in the family, putting you and other family members at the top where you belong.

If you like to train and you want a dog so you can be involved in dog activities and sports, the Aussie is perfect. Intelligent, trainable and athletic, Aussies excel in many fields of interest. Obviously, they were bred to be herding dogs and can be used for herding ducks, sheep or cattle. Aussies have excelled in obedience competition, agility, flyball and Frisbee competition. Aussies work as guide dogs, service dogs and therapy dogs. You name it, Aussies have done it.

If you decide to get an Australian Shepherd, you will need to dedicate a period of time daily to make sure your Aussie gets enough exercise. A walk cannot be considered adequate exercise for a healthy dog. Depending upon the dog's age and fitness level, exercise is a half an hour or forty-five minutes of throwing the Frisbee or tennis ball, or a two to three-mile run in an open field chasing rabbits. Exercise uses up excess energy, increases fitness and overall health and relieves stress both for you and your dog.

Do you want a dog that is watchful, alerting you to strangers yet not overpowering? Aussies are very alert and protective and will bark at the approach of strangers. Some Aussies have even been successful competitors in the sport of Schutzhund, which combines obedience, tracking and attack training. However, at

forty-five to sixty pounds, Aussies are medium sized, controllable and not overpowering for most dog owners.

Although most Aussie owners consider their dogs easy keepers, meaning they do not require a lot of grooming, you will need to be able to dedicate some time to caring for your dog. Aussies have a medium-length coat which should be thoroughly brushed at least once a week, although daily is better. Their coat will pick up burrs or foxtails (grass seeds) that must be removed from the coat. Depending on where you live, an Aussie coat can become the perfect habitat for fleas or ticks. Grooming also requires caring for the dog's feet, ears, teeth and overseeing the dog's overall health, all of which requires some of your time.

If you want an Aussie, you will have to ensure you have a safe place for it. *A securely fenced yard* is a must. Just as curiosity killed the proverbial cat, it has also killed many Aussies. Intelligent and curious, Aussies like to investigate and your Aussie must be protected from itself; clean up the garage, kitchen and bathroom, and put away any poisons, medicines or anything else that might be dangerous to an inquisitive dog.

Aussies are not good apartment dogs. Their working instincts, high energy level and need for exercise make them unsuited for most apartment dwellers unless you work at home and can devote time to several exercise excursions daily. If you do live in an apartment, do not despair. There are individual dogs within the breed that are naturally calmer than others and may be suited to a more confined life, you will simply have to search for that particular dog. In general, however, the breed is not suited to a sedentary lifestyle.

Making the decision to own a dog requires a financial commitment. There is obviously the initial purchase price to consider, as well as the initial trip to the veterinarian to make sure you have a healthy puppy, plus the series of vaccinations each puppy needs. You will also need to license the pup, spay or neuter it, have money in reserve for emergencies, pay for a dog training class and buy food and supplies. One dog owner kept track of her expenses and found it cost her over $1,200 per year in routine expenses to care for her adult dog. Those costs would increase for a puppy, or a geriatric dog, or any emergency medical bills.

Treadmill exercise is one way to keep city dogs fit.

If you have read this far and still want an Australian Shepherd, wonderful! With an Aussie, you will never be lonely or lacking for a friend. Loyal, devoted and intelligent with a quirky sense of humor and a love of play, an Aussie will be your companion for life and will fill your days with laughter.

Finding the Right Aussie for You.

A relationship between a dog and owner is just about as complicated as the relationships between husband and wife, parent and child or siblings. Just as each person is an individual, so is each dog, and to make a relationship work many factors come into play. Searching for the right dog may take some time and research so once you have decided to get an Aussie, do not rush out and bring home the first dog available.

Puppy or Adult Dog?

Decide first whether you want a puppy, an older pup or an adult dog. There are pros and cons to each. With a young puppy, from eight to twelve weeks of age, you will be able to raise it as you wish, controlling its socialization and training. This is an ideal age for human/puppy bonding and your puppy will form a strong emotional attachment. You will also have the work of raising the puppy, housetraining it and teaching it all the basic commands as well as waking up every three hours during the night for the first month or so.

An older puppy, from twelve weeks to seven months of age, may already be house-trained. A puppy this age might already know some of the basic commands, such as walking on a leash, sit and come. However, if the puppy has been raised in a kennel situation or a quiet backyard, it may not be socialized to the outside world or house-trained. You may have a lot of catch up work to do with an older puppy, and if it has not had enough contact with people, it may never catch up.

Many busy people prefer to adopt an adult dog. Mature dogs require less intensive care than do puppies, and if owned by responsible people, may have already learned the rules of living with people. An adult dog is usually less expensive to acquire and requires less financial investment initially, as it is probably already vaccinated and neutered. Adult dogs may take longer to adjust to a new household and may take longer to bond with you, but if the dog was a well-loved member of a family previously, it will settle in and become a member of your family.

An abused or neglected Aussie will require special handling. Although these dogs can often become great companions, it will take time and patience on your part. A very positive training program can help, emphasizing the dog's successes rather than its failures or mistakes. A neglected or abused Aussie should not be placed with a first-time dog owner, as it may be hard to control, may already have a number of bad habits or it may bite when cornered or afraid.

Male or Female?

The decision as to acquire a male or female puppy is primarily a personal one. Male Aussies are typically a little bigger and heavier boned with a harder, more aggressive personality. Bitches (females) are generally a little more refined in conformation and personality and tend to shed their coat after each heat cycle (generally every six months.) Both males and females are easily trained, both can be good at herding and stock dog work, in obedience or other activities, and, of course, both make exceptional companions.

If your dog is a pet or is not competing in conformation shows, you should have him or her altered. Male dogs are neutered (castrated.) By removing the testicles, the dog becomes unable to reproduce and many of the hormones that cause some of the common undesirable male characteristics—such as mounting, excessive leg-lifting, roaming and fighting—are removed. Neutered males are generally more affectionate toward their owners and more receptive to training than are intact males.

By spaying a bitch, the reproductive organs are removed and she will no longer go through her twice-yearly heat seasons. This will prevent unwanted puppies and the hassles associated with protecting a bitch in heat from unwanted suitors. Many people, dog owners and pet professionals, feel a spayed bitch is more tolerant toward children, and because of this is the preferred sex for most families.

Many dog owners are adamant in their preference for one sex over another. Some swear males are more affectionate, others feel bitches are. Some say males are more protective while others say bitches are. Many women say they can have a better relationship with a male dog, while men seem to be split—some like a big, masculine male dog and others say they have a better working relationship with a bitch. It is strictly a personal preference. If you are unsure, try to get to know some adult dogs owned by friends, even dogs of other breeds. Which sex appeals to you?

Where to Find an Aussie Puppy

The very best place to find a quality, healthy Australian Shepherd puppy is from an experienced breeder. You should never buy a puppy from a pet store, no matter how appealing a puppy in the window might look. Most pet stores buy their puppies from wholesale distributors who in turn buy their puppies from large scale dog farms, or puppy mills. The dogs are strictly breeding livestock and no consideration is taken of the dog's temperament, breed standard, health, soundness or suitability to breeding. Puppies are often taken from their mother and litter at five or six weeks of age (much too young!) so they can be shipped out and reach the stores by the time they are eight weeks old. Not only is this often unhealthy for the puppies but it can also leave lasting emotional scars, causing behavioral problems later.

Some pet stores try to bypass the puppy mills by buying their puppies from local breeders. Reputable breeders concerned about their dogs will not sell to pet stores because they want to make the decision about where their puppy ends up; they want to screen the potential owners and ensure their puppies live their lives in the best possible homes.

Before bringing your puppy home, be sure you have a securely fenced yard.

the premises, the breeder will have pictures and a pedigree to show you. She will have the mother's pedigree, registration papers, vaccination records and more. You should be able to see where the puppies are kept assess the cleanliness of their living space. The breeder should talk to you (not down to you) even if you are a beginner. The breeder should be willing to answer all your questions without hesitation. After all, she wants the puppies to go to good homes and will expect you to ask questions.

Because of this, pet stores cannot then buy the best puppies; they end up buying from either inexperienced breeders, people with accidental breedings, or from people who only desire to make a profit from breeding. In any case, you, the potential buyer of one of those puppies, will not have access to the parents of the litter. You cannot see the parents' temperament, conformation or health. You do not know how the mother was fed during gestation or lactation, how the puppies were cared for or when they were taken from the mother. There are entirely too many unanswered questions.

An experienced, reputable breeder who cares about her dogs and the breed in general will be able to answer all of your questions. You will be able to see the mother of the litter and if the stud dog (father) is not on

You can find a reputable breeder by asking around. Ask your veterinarian or local dog trainers. Many times the local animal shelter or Humane Society will maintain a list of local breeders. If they do not, they should have a list of local dog clubs, including the local Australian Shepherd club. Or go to dog shows in your area and look for healthy, well-behaved dogs and ask their owner whom they recommend. The Australian Shepherd Club of America also maintains a breeders list. (For a copy, write to the address listed in Appendix A.)

Once you find a couple of different breeders, call and make an appointment to talk to them. Ask breeders about their dogs; what do they do with them? Do they show in conformation? If you want a puppy that can compete in conformation dog shows, you will need to purchase a "show" puppy and a breeder experienced in this field can help you. If you want to work your new dog in herding trials or on a ranch, buy a puppy from a breeder who has dogs working in this area so you are assured of getting one with strong herding instincts and the temperament for the work.

Aussies can have a couple of different genetic health problems but most reputable breeders are working to avoid them. Ask to see the OFA (Orthopedic Foundation of America) certificates showing the breeding dogs are free from hip and elbow dysplasia. Ask also to see the CERF (Canine Eye registration Foundation) paperwork showing the breeding dogs are free from any eye defects.

Ask to see the breeder's facilities. Are the dogs clean and healthy? They should be bright-eyed and alert, and although protective barking is to be expected, they should settle down fairly quickly and be happy to see you and get attention from you. The facilities, the house, yard or kennel, should be clean and safe.

If you find a breeder with whom you can establish a relationship, find out when she will next have a litter and put your name on the waiting list. Sometimes breeders require a deposit, which may be nonrefundable should you change your mind.

Choosing the Right Puppy

When the breeder you have chosen has a litter of puppies available, tell her about yourself, what your personality is like, what your activity level is and what your goals are for this puppy. After all, she will be watching this litter from the time it is born and will know which puppy is more dominant or submissive, high energy or laid back, curious, withdrawn or shy. Let the breeder recommend two or three puppies she feels would suit you best; then you can chose from among those.

When choosing your puppy, do not grab the first puppy that runs up to you. Even though choosing a new puppy can be a very emotional decision, you need to make an informed, educated choice as much as possible so you get the puppy that is going to be right for you. The following six-step puppy test will help you make the best decision. The test has a number of different exercises you and the breeder can use to help determine which puppy is more or less dominant, which puppy has a strong natural retrieving instinct and which puppy accepts training willingly. The scoring section of the test deciphers the results for you, helping you to make the most informed decision. The test is best given when the puppy is between seven and nine weeks of age.

Attraction To People: *The pup came readily and climbed into your lap.*

Puppy Test

ATTRACTION TO PEOPLE

The puppy should be placed on the ground in a new area. Walk a few feet away and squat down. Call the puppy to you with a happy tone of voice, clapping your hands or patting the ground.

Circle the appropriate response:

A. The pup came readily, jumped on you and perhaps mouthed or bit your hands.

B. The pup came readily and climbed into your lap.

C. The pup came quickly, ears slightly back.

D. The pup came but was hesitant, may have crawled.

E. The pup did not come.

FOLLOWING

Stand up and walk away from the puppy, without encouraging it. Watch the pup's reactions.

Circle the appropriate response:

A. The pup followed closely, ears up, chased your feet.

B. Followed quickly, ears up, stayed close.

C. Followed hesitantly.

D. Followed slowly, may have crawled.

E. Did not follow.

Following: *Followed quickly, ears up, stayed close.*

RETRIEVE

Have a crumpled piece of paper and show it to the pup. When the pup sees it, toss it out a few feet in front of the pup.

Circle the appropriate response:

A. The pup chases after it quickly, brings it back but plays keep away, not giving it back.

B. The pup chases it, brings it back and allows you to take it.

C. The pup goes after it hesitantly, but does bring it at least part way back.

D. The pup does not go after it.

E. The pup goes after it but goes off in another direction.

Left, Retrieve: *Toss a crumpled piece of paper out in front of the pup...*
Above, Retrieve: *...the pup chases after it quickly...*
*Below, [*the pup*] brings it back and allows you to take it.*

Trainability: The pup sits quickly, its tail wagging.

TRAINABILITY

Standing up, with the pup looking at you, crumple the paper over its head, making a tantalizing noise, moving the paper and sound slowly toward the pup's tail. Tell the pup "sit" and praise it happily when it does, allowing the pup to play briefly with the paper. Repeat four or five times.

Circle the correct response:

A. The pup jumps on you for the paper.

B. The pup jumps on you the first time but then sits quickly, stub of its tail wagging, on the second or third try.

C. The pup sits on the second or third try.

D. The pup sits, then lays down.

E. The pup walks away.

SOCIAL HANDLING

Pet the puppy, stroking its head, down the neck, shoulders and back. Touch the ears, muzzle and feet. Rub your hands all over the pup.

Circle the appropriate response:

A. The puppy jumped at you, growled or bit at your hands.

B. The puppy pawed at your hands, wiggled, squirmed and tried to climb up the front of you.

C. The puppy wiggled and licked at your hands.

D. The pup rolled over, baring the belly.

E. The pup struggled and walked away.

Social Handling: The pup struggled and walked away.

Above, Social Handling: *Pet the puppy, stroking its head, down the neck, shoulders and back.*
Below, Dominance Down: *The pup did not struggle, licked at hands.*

DOMINANCE DOWN

On the ground, roll the puppy over onto its side or back and hold it still until it calms.

Circle the appropriate response:

A. The puppy struggled strongly, tried to bite, growled and cried.

B. The pup struggled strongly and may have cried.

C. The pup struggled, then calmed.

D. The pup did not struggle, licked at hands.

E. The pup did not struggle, may have urinated.

SCORING THE PUPPY

Three or more A's: This puppy is dominant and shows aggressive tendencies. It may bite. This is not a good pup for first time dog owners, for families with young children or for people with soft, passive or submissive personalities. This pup needs an adult household, with non-physical but firm training methods. Training methods that are too forceful or aggressive could cause this dog to fight back, becoming more aggressive. This dog might possibly be a good pet or working dog for an experienced, knowledgeable owner; however, it might also be a problem dog.

Three or more B's or a combination of all A's and B's: This puppy will tend to be outgoing and dominant. This pup is not good for first time dog owners or for families with young children, although older kids would probably be okay. This could be a good working dog for an experienced owner.

Three or more C's: This dog will adapt to most households and should be suitable for families with children, the elderly or first time dog owners. This dog should take well to training.

Three or more D's: This submissive dog will need kind and gentle handling but could be a good companion for a senior citizen or a quiet adult. Positive training methods and careful socialization can integrate this dog into society. This dog needs to be protected from rough handling.

Three or more E's or a combination of D's and E's: This dog may be anti-social or shy. If this pup also has an A in its ratings, it may bite when faced with stressful situations. This is not a good puppy for children or inexperienced dog owners.

If you are unsure of your results or feel that the puppy has scored a conglomeration of scores that make no sense, then repeat the test in a new location. You might feel more comfortable doing it a second time anyway. Or you may want to ask someone else to repeat the test so that you can watch and then compare scores.

NOT INFALLIBLE

This, and any other puppy test, is to be used to help you select a puppy, however the tests are not infallible. There are still many other factors to be taken into consideration, including your emotional response to the puppy. The puppy's scores are also not set in concrete. Behavior can change with training, socialization and maturity. However, with these limitations in mind, a puppy test can

increase the odds so that you choose the right puppy for you.

Once you have narrowed your choices, you will need to consider each puppy's health. A healthy puppy will be bright-eyed and alert. It will move freely, without any limping. Snap your fingers behind the puppy. Does it show any reaction to the sound? Test its vision. Does it follow your hand in motion? The puppy's coat will be fuzzy, thick and should be relatively clean. There should be no sores, scabs, scales or bald spots. There should be no stools or diarrhea caked around the anus, nor should there be any nasal discharge or matter in the eyes. The ears should be clean, the teeth white and the gums pink and firm. When you put your hands on the puppy, it should feel firm and solid. When you pick it up, it should feel heavier than it looks.

Once you have chosen the puppy you want and the breeder agrees with your choice, it is time to get down to business. Most breeders offer a limited guarantee for their puppies, often requiring you take the puppy to your veterinarian within forty-eight hours of buying it to guarantee the puppy is in good health at the time. This visit is for your protection as well as for your breeder. The veterinarian will look over the pup to make sure it is healthy and will get your puppy started on its shots, coordinating its schedule with the vaccination record that your breeder gave you.

Many breeders will guarantee the puppy is free from any serious defects, such as hip dysplasia, blindness or deafness. If you are buying a conformation show prospect puppy, the breeder may guarantee the puppy is free from any disqualifying faults but it is impossible to guarantee that any given puppy will "win" or finish its championship.

The breeder should write you a bill of sale at the time of the puppy's purchase. This bill of sale or contract should spell out the entire purchase agreement. If you are buying a pet puppy (not for show) the breeder may agree to issue you the registration papers once your puppy is spayed or neutered. The AKC also issues a "Limited Registration" provision. If the breeder sells you a puppy as a "pet" puppy, she may sign a line on the registration papers that indicates this, and the puppy then cannot be used for breeding; or if it is, the resulting puppies cannot be registered. If you are buying a show puppy, the breeder might remain on the papers as a co-owner until the dog or bitch has been bred a specific number of times. No matter what the agreement, make sure all parts of the contract are agreeable to you and to your breeder, and that everything is in writing.

The breeder might give you one or more sets of registration papers that will have to be signed by you and sent in to the proper registry to register the dog in your name. Australian Shepherds can be registered with several different registries. The Australian Shepherd Club of America (ASCA) is the predominant organization for American Aussies. ASCA awards conformation championships, obedience, tracking and titles, and stockdog certificates. The American Kennel Club (AKC) also registers Aussies and awards conformation, obedience, performance and herding titles. The United Kennel Club (UKC) recognizes Aussies in its obedience program and the National Stock Dog Registry also registers Aussies. Your breeder may sign over to you registration papers from any one or all of the above registries. The breeder should also give you, with the registration papers, a three, four, or five-generation pedigree detailing your puppy's ancestors.

Ch. Moonlights Roll Over Beethoven, Black-tri.

Choosing an Adult Dog

If you decide an adult dog is better for you now, there are many different places to look. Most regional Australian Shepherd clubs operate rescue services, placing Aussies given up by their owners. The dogs might have been given up for a number of reasons; perhaps a young military family was going overseas or an elderly owner passed away. Most rescue groups know something of the dog's background and screen it carefully for health or behavioral problems. Sometimes a donation is requested to cover the group's costs for vaccinating, neutering or bathing the dog.

Many times breeders will have a young adult dog to place. Maybe it was initially kept as a potential show prospect that did not work out, or the breeder decided she had too many dogs. Occasionally a puppy that a breeder sold will come back for some reason; the original home was not working out. Humane Societies and animal shelters will also have Aussies once in a while.

When choosing an adult dog, the guidelines are the same no matter where you find it. Make sure, first of all, that the dog is healthy. The guidelines for checking the dog's health are basically the same as for a puppy. The dog should have clear, bright eyes with no discharge, clean ears, white, clean teeth and a healthy coat with no scabs or bald spots. It should move easily, with no limping and when you run your hands over it there should be no sore spots or flinching.

Observe the dog's behavior. Does it have any bad habits you are not prepared to deal with? Does it jump on people? Pull on the leash? Is it housetrained? Does it attempt run away? All of these problems can be handled, but you must have the desire, time and energy.

If you are lucky, you may even find an adult that has had some training. Ask the dog to sit and see if it recognizes the word. Take the leash, put the dog on your left side and as you start to walk, ask the dog to heel. How does it respond? Ask the people who have been caring for the dog if this is a dog they

WTCH Ramblin Rose Texas Gambler RDX

"Gambler"

OWNER: GEORGE FREY
BREEDER: JOANN FREY

Within six weeks of beginning stockdog training, Gambler knew left and right like he'd been born with the knowledge; in fact, Gambler was so easy to train George said, "he'd be a hard act to follow." Gambler lives to work for George, following him around all day just waiting for something to do, waiting for a chance to work.

George entered Gambler in a stockdog trial after watching a neighbor work one of Gambler's littermates. On their first time out, Gambler qualified six out of six times. They were on their way.

At the 1989 ASCA National Specialty Stockdog Trials, Gambler's third trial, he competed in the open class and tied three advanced dogs for high in trial. When the run-off was completed, Gambler had won second place. Gambler has since gone on to compete in the ASCA National Finals in ducks, sheep and cattle in 1990, 1991, 1992 and 1993. Although Gambler has gone on to win numerous high in trial awards, George is proudest of the fact that Gambler is one of the top dogs in the nation.

Gambler is not all work, though; he loves to play. He has competed in the local Frisbee competitions, placing or winning every year. He will chase a stick until George is too tired to throw it, and he can get the squeaky out of a toy faster than you can pay for it!

would be willing to keep if they were looking for a dog and then ask them to elaborate. Why would they? Or why not?

Before you commit yourself to an unknown Aussie, make sure you can take the dog to your veterinarian prior to formalizing any agreement. Have your veterinarian go over the dog thoroughly. If it has some behavioral problems you have questions about, ask a dog trainer to meet the dog and get her opinion. With these professionals helping you, you will be better able to make an informed decision.

CHAPTER 3

Bringing Home
Your New Aussie

❖⟞═══⟝ ⟝═══⟞❖

YOU ARE GOING to need to go shopping before you bring home your new puppy. Dog food, of course, is a necessity. Call the breeder and ask what kind of food your puppy has been eating so you can keep it on the same food. If you want to feed a different brand later, you can change it gradually over a period of a couple of weeks so the puppy does not get an upset stomach and diarrhea from an abrupt change. You will need a food bowl and unspillable water bowl; stainless steel is unbreakable, unchewable and the easiest to clean. You may want to have a water bowl in the house as well as one outside.

Your puppy is going to need a place to call its own. The best bed you can get your puppy is a dog crate. A crate is a plastic, metal or wire travel cage and will serve as its bed and place of refuge. Get one that will be big enough for your pup to stand up and turn around in when it's full grown. If you have no idea, ask your breeder to recommend a size. Later on in this chapter we will tell you how to use the crate properly.

You will need a leash and a buckle-type collar so your Aussie can start learning how to walk on a leash. While you are shopping for collars, you may want to get two or three

A 300 or 400 crate is the correct size for an Aussie. Crates are commonly manufactured in plastic, steel or wire.

of increasing sizes because your puppy will outgrow them rapidly. Order an identification tag for your Aussie right away, one with the puppy's name, your name and telephone number and immediately attach it to the buckle collar.

Toys are a necessity for all puppies. If you do not have appropriate toys for your Aussie to chew on and play with, it will find something—like your expensive shoes. Clean, bleached rawhides (made in the United States, not overseas) are good for teething puppies as long as the puppy is not biting off big chunks it might choke on or swallow. The same applies to hard rubber toys or squeaky toys.

You will also need a metal comb and a stiff brush, some mild shampoo suitable for puppies and a supply of towels, both for bathing, cleaning up, and for the puppy's bed.

If you have adopted or purchased an adult dog, you will need basically the same supplies, except you may need a training collar for walking and training as well as the buckle collar for everyday use.

Stages of Puppy Development

Before you bring your Aussie home, it is important to understand the stages of development puppies go through so you are prepared to deal with these changes as the puppy grows. These stages of development and what happens (or does not happen) to the puppy will have a lasting effect on its behavior in adult life.

From birth to three weeks of age, your Aussie puppy is helpless. Its needs are centered on its mother and she provides everything the puppy needs: food, warmth and security. The dam (the mother dog, or bitch) should be allowed to care for the pups with limited interference from people.

At four weeks of age the puppy's needs are still provided by its mother but as it gets stronger, the puppy and its littermates will begin their first attempts at play. During this stage, your Aussie's mental development is increasing. The breeder should provide safe, simple toys for the puppies to climb on and investigate.

During the fifth through seventh weeks of life, the puppy is growing rapidly and learning to walk and run with more coordination. Your puppy's mental processes are increasing, too, and it will learn to recognize people and will begin to respond to individual voices. The breeder's family

One week.

Three weeks.

Five weeks.

members can hold the puppies, stroke them, touch their toes and so on, but the breeder should make sure the handling is calm and quiet so that the puppies are not frightened by the attention.

During this stage of development, the dam will begin disciplining the puppies and she should not be interfered with as she does this. Her initial corrections are vitally important to your puppy's later acceptance of your dominance, discipline and training. For example, if one of her puppies bites her too hard, her correction is short and sharp: a growl and muzzle bite that stops as soon as the puppy reacts submissively. The correction is always followed by love and affection and she never holds a grudge.

Your puppy's littermates will teach it a lot at this age, too, and for that reason the puppy should never go to a new home now. As the puppies wrestle and play with each other, they learn how to get along with other dogs: how to play, what play is too rough, when to be submissive and what to take seriously.

This stage is a good time for the breeder to introduce the puppy to the family cat and other pets provided these visits are carefully supervised and, if the dam appears worried, remove the other pet.

The eighth week of life is a fearful time. Although this is traditionally when most puppies go to their new homes, you will be much better off waiting one more week. Anything that frightens your puppy now could have lasting effects. If the car ride home frightens the puppy or it gets carsick, it can be afraid of the car for a long time and will probably continue to get sick. If the puppy goes to the veterinarian's office right away and is hurt by the vaccination, it will remember that, too.

One week in the life of a puppy can make a big difference, and at nine or ten weeks of age, your Aussie is ready to go home with you. This is when the puppy is best able to form strong emotional attachments to people, so take advantage of this and plan on spending a lot of time with your new puppy over the next couple of weeks.

Your Aussie's pack instincts are developing now, too, and the puppy should

Eight weeks.

be handled by all of the family members and meet the family pets. Gentle, positive training can start now and household rules should be introduced.

At ten to twelve weeks of age, discipline becomes more important. Make sure household rules are established and enforced. Do not allow your puppy to do things now that you are not going to want it to do later, such as jumping on people, climbing on the furniture or stealing food. Do not allow your puppy to have free run of the house, either. Freedom is a privilege to be earned by good behavior.

At this age, your Aussie's mental capacities are developing. All the puppy lacks is experience and an increased attention span. A puppy kindergarten class would be a great experience now, allowing the puppy to socialize with other puppies and learning to behave in public with lots of distractions.

From thirteen to sixteen weeks of age your puppy will begin testing its place in your family pack, so training is important as is socialization. Make sure everyone in the family is enforcing the household rules consistently. The puppy's flight instinct is also

Your puppy should be introduced to other members of the household, and all introductions should be supervised.

developing, causing it to run from real or imaginary threats. Keep it on leash when outside the house so you do not lose your puppy should it run.

Your Aussie's training should be positive at this age. Use lots of praise, petting and treats to encourage a happy attitude toward training. A four-month-old puppy is past the most critical periods of development, but it cannot be considered grown up either mentally or physically. Training and investigating new things should continue for the puppy's mental growth, as should socialization. The world can be either a scary place or it can be an adventure: your puppy's attitude will be a reflection of your own.

Adolescence, which usually begins at about seven or eight months of age, can be a very trying time. The puppy can be compared to a human adolescent of thirteen to fourteen years of age. The teenaged Aussie will test your dominance and the household rules to see if they are really going to be enforced. Rules that were previously well known such as, "stay off the sofa" will be ignored, and known obedience commands such as, "sit" will bring a blank, uncomprehending look or even outright defiance. All of these things do not mean your Aussie is bad or stupid; rather, it means your dog is normal. Like human teenagers, it will grow up. Eventually.

Now that you have chosen your new puppy, have the equipment it needs, and understand the stages of development it will go through, you are ready to bring it home.

Most adult dogs will quickly accept a new puppy.

Getting Started Right

Give your puppy a few days to settle into your household and learn your voice, walk, schedule and habits before you start introducing it to other people. The puppy's first day home is not the time to show it off to your friends and all the neighbors, but it is time to start setting some basic household rules.

Housetraining

Puppies thrive on a schedule and a regular routine will help tremendously with housetraining. Feed it at the same time every morning and evening, give midday snacks at the same time each day, and take it on walks at a regular time. Schedule trips outside so your Aussie can relieve itself after waking up from a nap, after playing, after eating and about every two hours in between.

Make sure you go outside with your puppy, otherwise you will not know whether it has relieved itself or not and you will lose a valuable opportunity to praise it. Go out with your puppy and tell it, "Aussie, go potty." (Use a vocabulary you are comfortable with.) Do not play with it now, just stand around ignoring it until it goes. When the puppy squats to urinate or move its bowels, wait until it is just about finished and then tell it, "Good dog to go potty!" in a happy, joyful tone of voice.

Limit your Aussie's freedom in the house. Too much freedom gives the puppy too many opportunities to have housetraining accidents or to get into other trouble such as chewing up shoes, getting into the trash cans or pulling the tablecloth off of the table. Instead, keep your puppy close to you, keeping an eye on it, and limit its freedom. If you can not watch the puppy, put it outside in the yard (if it is securely fenced) or put it in its crate.

At the beginning of this chapter, you were told to buy your new puppy a crate. A crate will help with your Aussie's house-training by confining it when you can not supervise it and by teaching the puppy to hold its bowels and bladder, as most puppies do not want to soil their bed. Your Aussie should sleep in its crate, not in your bed or with the kids. Your puppy needs its own place

where it can relax, away from the bustle of the household. The crate can be a refuge from boisterous children or a safe place to curl up when it is tired or sick. The best place for the crate is next to your bed. Move your night stand out and put your alarm clock on top of the crate. This way your puppy can be close to you, see you and smell you all night, rather than being exiled to the laundry room or bathroom.

Introduce your new puppy to the crate right away. After all, it was confined to a whelping box with its mother, so it is already used to some restrictions. Toss a treat into the crate and, leaving the door open, allow the puppy to run in, get the treat and come back out. Do this several times. When your Aussie is running in and out with no hesitation, feed it in the crate, closing the door behind it. Let the puppy out as soon as it finishes eating.

When you go to bed, take your Aussie outside and tell it to go potty, then bring it to your bedroom and put the puppy in its crate. Then go to bed yourself. If the pup starts to cry, thump on the top of the crate and tell it to be quiet. Expect some whining and restlessness the first night; it has never been away from its mother and littermates. Because you are near and it is not alone, it should settle down quickly.

Expect the puppy to have to go outside to relieve itself once or twice during the night for the first couple of weeks. It needs to mature a little physically and learn bladder control before it can sleep through night. For the same reason, never leave the puppy in the crate for more than four hours at a time, except at night when you are close enough to wake up if it cries.

Social Handling

Right away, start teaching your Aussie to allow you to touch every part of its body so you can take care of it. Sit on the floor and lay your puppy in your lap, cradled between your

Give your puppy plenty of exercise and toys to play with to keep it entertained and help avoid destructive behavior.

An Aussie can be trained to get along with any other family pets.

legs. Run your hands over its body, starting at its head, touching its ears, running your hands over the eye lids. Open the puppy's mouth and look at those needle-sharp baby teeth. Give a little puppy massage as you run your hands down its neck to the shoulders, down the legs, touching the paws and toe nails. Continue in this manner until you have touched every square inch of its body.

There are several benefits to this exercise, besides the obvious benefit of being able to touch the puppy to take care of it. By giving this little massage, you are also relaxing your puppy. This can work to your benefit if you come home to a wired, excited puppy. Instead of wrestling with it, give it a massage. This exercise is also a good time to bond with your puppy, teaching it to trust your hands. And last, as an additional benefit, by positioning yourself above the puppy as it is laying still for this exercise, you are putting yourself in the dominant position, which will help maintain (or establish) your dominant position in the family in relation to your Aussie.

Give Your Aussie a Job

Getting Aussie started right means you need to give your puppy a job right away. Do not have it do anything harder than it is capable of, but the puppy does need to learn to work for you.

Start by teaching it to sit. Let your Aussie see and smell that you have a treat in your hand, then tell it "Aussie, sit!" At the same time, move the treat back toward its hips over its head so the puppy looks up and back to follow your hand. This will be uncomfortable, so the puppy will sit. As soon as its rump hits the ground, praise "Good puppy!" and give the treat.

If your puppy does not follow this method well, an alternative way to teach it to sit is to put your hands on the puppy's body and as you say "Sit," shape it into position. The problem with using your hands is that some puppies learn "sit" means "Let my owner shape me into the sit," instead of doing it themselves.

Once your Aussie knows the sit command, start having it sit for everything it wants. This is going to be its job for a while. Your puppy can sit for treats, breakfast, dinner and for chew toys. Have it sit before you pet it. The puppy can sit before you hook up the leash to go for a walk and it can sit before you open the door for it to go outside or to come in. This exercise is very simple and something ten-to-twelve-week-old puppies can learn right away and it also gives the puppy a very strong message: the puppy is working for you, and you are the giver of the things it wants.

Household Rules

Set up household rules now while your puppy is still young so you can avoid problems later and then make sure everyone in the house abides by the rules. If one person enforces the rules but other people do not, your Aussie will be confused and will never be reliable. When you set up the rules, have a family meeting so everyone has a say in the decision and everyone agrees with the final outcome.

In deciding upon the rules, do not think of your puppy now, but instead think of the dog as it will become. It may not bother you to have it on the furniture now, but are you still going to want it up there when your dog is full grown? Are you going to want it begging from the table? Or jumping on guests?

Keep in mind, too, what some of the puppy's (and your) actions are conveying. You may think it is innocent fun when your puppy dashes up the stairs and then turns around to see if you are following but in reality, what is happening is that the puppy dashes up the stairs so it can turn around and watch you follow with lowered eyes. In other words, at the top of the stairs your dog is the dominant dog. So teach your puppy to wait and walk up the stairs behind you.

Do not let your Aussie dash ahead of you through doors, either; that is just as bad. When your puppy comes nudging your hand

Puppies enjoy vinyl toys that make squeaky noises. They come in various shapes, sizes and textures, but be sure to choose a toy that will not tear into pieces your puppy can swallow or choke on.

In addition to a securely fenced yard, your Aussie will need a weather-proof house.

for you to pet it, do not do it right away, instead, have it sit first, then pet it. And in the same vein, always eat before you feed your puppy. Eat your breakfast first, then feed it. In the natural world of dogs and other related canines, the dominant dog or wolf always eats first, then the submissive ones eat the leftovers. You do not need to give your puppy your leftovers, however, the timing of your meals will communicate the same message.

We Are Made for Each Other

Dogs and people have been partners for at least twelve thousand years, that we know of anyway. Some researchers think the relationship might even be twenty-five to a hundred thousand years old. Both our species are very social, which is why we are so perfect for each other. People live in family groups and communities. Dogs live in packs and although our families are very different from packs, they are similar enough that dogs can be comfortable with us. Over the centuries people have selectively bred dogs, producing herding dogs, such as the Australian Shepherd, working dogs, hunting dogs and companion dogs. These dogs helped humankind survive.

People also bred for personalities and breeds that would bond closely with humans. This bond made it easier to train dogs and it also made it easier to develop the emotional relationship that makes owning a dog so special. Although the tendency to bond with people is hereditary in dogs, the bond itself is not and must be relearned with each new puppy. That special relationship between a dog and its owner does not happen automatically. It takes patience, time, training and love. But once the bond is formed, there is nothing like it.

Always curious, Aussies want to be part of every family activity.

CHAPTER 4

Training Your Australian Shepherd

THROUGHOUT OUR HISTORY dogs have been bred to work for us. Dogs pulled or carried loads, tracked, located, flushed or caught game, herded domestic animals or guarded us from predators or our enemies. Although we valued dogs' companionship, during much of our history, humanity was too poor to feed an animal that did not work for its keep so the only dogs kept or bred were those that had proved their value.

As dogs and humanity grew and our societies changed, we learned to train our dogs so that we used more than just the dogs' instincts to aid us. A dog that herded domestic animals, for example, could also be taught to pull a load and to guard children from danger. Training became a skill and a dog that had good working instincts and could be trained to do additional tasks became even more valuable.

Today, well-trained dogs have benefits that are not allowed their untrained cousins. A well-behaved dog is welcome in the house even when the family is eating, because it has been taught not to beg under the table. The trained dog is not exiled to the backyard when guests come over; instead the dog greets the guests without jumping on them and then lays quietly at its owner's feet. The well-trained dog can go for walks without

55

pulling its owner, and it can be trusted not to jump on the neighbors. The trained dog can participate in many activities, for competition and for fun. Instead of being shut in the backyard all the time, the well-trained dog is a member of the family.

How Does Your Aussie Learn?

All creatures that are capable of learning, learn in a similar manner. Simply stated, we tend to avoid what is unpleasant and we will repeat something that causes pleasure. When we smell the fragrance of a flower, we learn that a flower of that petal pattern, shape and coloring smells good and when we see that particular flower again, we will stick our nose in it, so that we can again enjoy its fragrance. If, when we smelled that flower, a bee was gathering pollen and we got stung, we would have learned to avoid that flower or to at least look carefully for stinging insects before sniffing.

Dogs learn in much the same way and we can use this to teach them; in fact, many people use it without realizing they are doing so. If you give your Aussie a treat for coming to you when you call, you are teaching it that it is a good thing to come to you. If you scold the dog when it comes to you, perhaps for chewing up your couch cushion, you are teaching it to avoid you when you say the word "come." If you flea spray your dog after calling it to come, you are teaching it that nasty things happen when you call it.

Communication is one of the keys to training; not necessarily what you think you are communicating to your dog but what

your dog is actually understanding. For example, if your dog is barking at another dog, instead of correcting it for barking, you tell it (using a reassuring tone of voice), "That dog is okay. Don't bark. He won't hurt you," you have not told your dog that barking at other dogs is bad. Instead your reassuring tone of voice told it that what it was doing— barking at the other dog—was right. You communicated exactly the opposite of what you wanted. Try to look at what you are saying, and how you are saying it, from your Aussie's point of view.

While training your Aussie, you will use a lot of positive reinforcements: verbal praise, petting, food treats and play. Simply saying the words "Good dog" are not important to your dog; instead, it is the tone of voice you use when you say them. Use the same tone of voice that you used as a kid when you said, "Ice cream!" Do not be afraid to be enthusiastic!

When you pet your Aussie to reinforce good behavior, the petting should be something the dog likes. Some dogs enjoy a good thump on the ribs while others like their ears rubbed, and some like their chest scratched. These positive reinforcements, because they are something your dog wants, motivate it to concentrate and to do what you want, rather than what the dog would rather do on its own. Positive reinforcements also keep the training fun, both for you and for your dog.

When your Aussie makes a mistake or when it is doing something that you do not want it to do, use something the dog dislikes to stop it or to make it uncomfortable for it to continue. For example, if your Aussie barks

too much at the front window when neighborhood kids are outside playing, you can teach your dog to stop by first telling it, "Aussie, quiet!" If it ignores you (which it will probably do) then squirt it quickly with a squirt bottle filled with water and a touch of vinegar. It will not hurt your dog, but the odor of the vinegar will offend its sense of smell (its most important sense) and it will stop barking to wipe its nose or to sneeze. When the dog stops barking, you can then praise it: "Good dog to be quiet!"

What you have done is: 1. Given your Aussie a command to be quiet. 2. When it ignored you, you squirted it to interrupt the barking. 3. When it stopped, you praised it for stopping. By using this interruption, followed by praise, you made your dog listen to you so that it could learn and you eliminated the need to continue yelling, getting louder and louder as it continued to bark and ignore you. After two or three interruptions like this, you will find that your Aussie will stop barking on your first command and you will no longer need the squirt bottle.

The squirt bottle will work when you need to correct your dog and you do not have the leash on it. Jumping on the screen door, stealing slippers, nipping at your heels and of course, barking, are all easily corrected with the squirt bottle.

You can use a leash on your Aussie to control it, physically, and it can also be used to give a correction or act as an interruption. Use the leash when you are out for a walk or outside of your fenced yard. You can also use the leash in the house. If you can keep an eye on your Aussie to make sure it does not get it tangled, let it drag the leash when it is in the house with you so that you can teach and enforce the household rules.

Your voice can also serve as an interruption or a correction. Use a deep, growly tone of voice. "Acck! That's enough!" Always use your voice when you give any kind of correction—squirt bottle or leash—because you want to teach your dog to pay attention to you, and eventually you want to be able to control your dog verbally without having to rely on the leash or other props. Your voice is your most important training tool; use it lavishly to praise the dog, to interrupt bad behavior and to correct it.

The Basic Commands

There are several basic commands that all well-trained dogs must understand. These include: heel (walk on a leash without pulling), sit, down, stay, watch me, come and the retrieve. Additional commands can be taught, depending upon your needs and your household routine.

SIT

The first command that all dogs need to learn is the sit. Sit is the foundation for everything else because it puts your dog in one spot and requires it to think about what it is doing. Your dog cannot sit and bounce around at the same time. When it is sitting, you can get your Aussie's attention and give it additional commands or directions.

Teach the sit by first attaching your Aussie's leash to its collar. With your dog on your left side, place your right hand on the front of your dog's neck at about collar height. Tell your dog, "Aussie, sit," and at the same time push up and back with your right hand on its neck as your left hand slides down its back toward the tail, pressing down slightly at the hips. If you think of your dog's body as a see-saw, you can picture this. Up and back at the neck, down at the hips.

When your Aussie's hips hit the ground, keep your right hand at the collar and with your left hand pet your dog, telling it, "Good dog to sit!" If it tries to pop back up, tell your dog, "Acck! No! Sit!" and reposition it. When you are ready for it to get back up, pat it on the shoulder or ribcage and tell your dog, "Aussie, Release! Good dog," and encourage it

to get up. Just as we want your Aussie to learn that "sit" means lower your hips to the ground and be still, we want it to learn that "release" means you are all done with what we were doing, you can move now.

Again, the process for teaching the sit is: 1. Right hand in front of your Aussie's neck. 2. Give the command, "Aussie, sit," as you push slightly up and back with the right hand and down and back with the left hand, at the hips. 3. When your dog sits, pet with the left hand, keeping the right hand at the collar, praising "Good dog!" 4. When you are ready for your Aussie to move, say, "Aussie, release!" and pat it on the shoulder, encouraging it to move.

The Sit: *Push up and back with your right hand under the dog's neck as your left hand slides down its back toward the tail, pressing down slightly at the hips.*

Make sure you tell your dog to sit only once and then follow through and make it sit. Do not tell your dog, "Aussie, Sit. Sit. Sit. Sit, please SIT" One command and follow through. Then, once your Aussie knows the sit and is doing it reliably, stop using your left hand. Keep your right hand on the dog until it is sitting one hundred percent of the time, on your first command.

In the previous chapter, we talked about having your puppy sit for everything it wants. Have it sit for a treat, a ball or squeaky toy and sit for its meals. Have your dog sit before you hook up the leash to go for a walk and have your dog sit before you pet it. This exercise is good for all dogs, not just puppies. By having your dog sit for everything, it learns that it works for you. This is a very important message for all dogs, but especially dogs bred to work, like the Australian Shepherd.

WATCH ME

The "watch me" teaches your dog to focus on you. By learning a command that means "pay attention to me" you can have your dog pay attention to you in distracting circumstances: when a dog is barking behind a fence as you walk by, when a child dashes by on a skateboard, when you are walking in a crowd and so on. When your Aussie is paying attention and looking at you as you are walking, it cannot be dragging you down the street—it is physically impossible for the dog to do both. As a result, this can be a very important and useful command.

Start by having your Aussie sit. With a treat in your right hand, show it to your dog and let it smell the treat. Tell your dog "Watch me," and move your hand with the treat toward your face. Initially, your dog is going to watch your hand because you are taking the treat away. As your hand approaches your chin, watch your dog's eyes and when it looks at your face, immediately praise it, "Good dog to watch me!" and pop the treat in its mouth. Always praise before you give it the treat because although it is watching you now because of the treat, eventually

Watch Me: Tell your dog "watch me" and move your hand with the treat toward your face.

you will get rid of the treats and when you do, you want the dog working for your verbal praise.

When your Aussie is watching you reliably when sitting in front of you, start backing away from the dog as you encourage it to walk. As you back away, have your dog follow, face-to-face, as you do another "watch me." This teaches your dog that it can watch you and walk at the same time. When your dog will watch you as you back up a few feet at a time, make it more challenging, backing up in a zigzag pattern.

When your Aussie can follow you as you back up in turns and circles, have it do a "watch me" and walk on your left side at the same time, encouraging the dog to walk with you as you change pacc—slow and fast, and making turns. Use the treat as much as you need, going back and forth from your Aussie's nose to your chin. Emphasize the praise when your dog does it right: "Yeah! Good dog! Super!"

HEEL

When your Aussie can walk on your left side and watch you, it is time to teach the heel command. "Heel" means, to your dog, walk by my left side, shoulder by my leg, without pulling, staying with me as I walk, slow, fast or turn; which is exactly what we have been having it do. Because you will not want to walk your Aussie for the rest of its natural life, bent over, with a treat in hand, doing a "watch me," it will need to understand the "heel" command.

Start by sitting your dog on your left side. Have the leash in your left hand and your treat in your right hand. Tell your Aussie, "Watch me." Then when it does, say "Aussie, heel," and start walking forward at a natural, comfortable pace for you. If your dog is walking with you, paying attention to you, praise it. If the dog charges ahead, snap the leash back and tell it, in a deep, growly tone of voice, "Acckk! No pull!" and then follow the correction with a "Watch me" in a positive tone of voice.

Concentrate on your timing. Praise your dog when it is walking with you in the position you want. Correct your dog when it moves from that position and follow each correction with a "Watch me" to show the dog what it is that you want it to do and where you want it to walk. Initially, you will go back and forth between "Watch me," praise, and corrections and you may feel silly, but it all helps your Aussie learn.

Heel: *Have your dog walk by your left side, without pulling or falling behind.*

DOWN

The "down" is a very useful command, especially when combined with the "stay," which will be explained next. When your Aussie is given the "down/stay" commands, it must lay down and be still for a period of time. Initially, this may be for just two or three seconds, but with practice it can be increased to twenty or thirty minutes, even an hour. This means your Aussie can lay down and be still while you eat dinner or talk with guests, or while you talk to neighbors out in front of the house. You can tell it to lay down and stay while you are watching television or while you are reading your child a bedtime story. The command "down" has dozens of uses.

The DOWN: *From a sitting position, pull the front legs out and down.*

Teach the "down" by first having your dog sit. Show your Aussie the treat you are holding in your right hand while at the same time your left hand holds its collar. Tell your dog, "Aussie, down" as you take your right hand with the treat straight down to the ground in front of its feet and your left hand pulls its collar toward the ground, encouraging the dog to lay down. As your dog lays down, praise it and give it the treat. Do not let it pop back up on its own. When you are ready for it to get up, release your dog as you do from the sit: "Aussie, release!" and pat it on the shoulder. When your dog is starting to go down on its own, stop using your left hand on its collar but continue using the hand signal with the treat.

If your Aussie does not lay down when you signal with the treat, there is an alternative technique you can use. Again, with your dog sitting, tell your dog, "Aussie, down," and pull the front legs out and down so your dog lays down. Praise it for laying down even though you actually positioned it, and when you are ready for the dog to move, release it, "Aussie, release!"

STAY

The "stay" command will be used with both the "sit" and the "down" commands. We want "stay" to mean "Don't move from this position until I come back to you and release you," which means you should never tell your Aussie to stay and then go off and forget about it. Also, never tell your dog to stay for longer than it is capable of doing at that stage of training. In the beginning, it may only be capable of holding a stay for a few seconds. As it gains confidence you can increase the time.

With your Aussie in a sit by your left side, place your hand in front of your dog's face and tell it "Aussie, stay," and take one or two steps away, no farther. Count "One Mississippi, two Mississippi, three" and go back to it, praising your dog while it is still sitting and then release it. Do not let your dog release itself as you walk back or as you praise it. If your dog moves while you are away, or while you are praising it, correct it by snapping the leash and giving it a verbal correction, "Acckk!" and then placing it back in position.

When your dog learns to hold the stay for a few seconds, gradually increase the time and distance. If your Aussie starts to make mistakes, mover closer and shorten the time you are asking it to stay. Practice for a time and at a distance that the dog is comfortable with until it is capable of doing it well, then gradually increase the time and distance, working back up to where it was before. Always make certain your Aussie experiences success during these exercises.

Teach the "down/stay" in the same manner. In fact, mix up the exercises, do a "sit/stay" one time and a "down/stay" the next. Your Aussie will be able to do a much longer "down/stay" than a "sit/stay" because the "down/stay" is more comfortable and takes less effort.

Opposite and Above, The Sit and Down Stay: *With your dog by your left side, place your hand in front of your dog's face and tell it, "stay."*

COME

Your Aussie needs to learn that "come" means to go directly to you whenever you call it, every time you call it and to ignore any and all distractions along the way. This means if the ball goes in the street, the dog must for-get about the ball and go directly to you when you call. Obviously, this command can be a lifesaver but it can also make life much nicer on a day-to-day basis. If your Aussie comes to you every time you call, you are saved the effort of chasing it when you want it to come inside, go outside, when you want to brush your dog or put the leash on it.

To get a good, reliable "come" response, there are some important points to keep in mind. First, as we mentioned earlier, you must always keep the come command positive. Never, ever call your Aussie to come and then do something negative to it. Never call your dog to come and then flea spray it or bathe it. Never call your dog to come and then punish it for something that it did earlier. You may think you are punishing it for chewing up a couch cushion three hours ago but your dog is going to associate the punishment with the last thing that happened, which was you calling it to come.

Keep the "come" positive by always praising the dog for coming to you, even if it was simply across the yard or across the room. Use a happy, "Ice cream!" tone of voice, "Good dog to come! Super!" Pet your dog, pop a treat in its mouth or toss its favorite toy. Make a big deal out of the "come" so that your dog learns that the very best thing it can do is come to you.

You can also practice the "come" using the leash. With your dog on the leash, simply back away from it and call it to come. If your dog does not respond right away, snap the leash so that you get its attention and repeat the command, using the leash to enforce it. Even though you will use the leash to make sure that your Aussie does come to you, keep praising it at the same time. Do not scold your dog or correct it verbally or it could associate that scolding with coming to you. Remember, you may understand what you are doing but your dog may not. Keep misunderstandings to a minimum.

RETRIEVE

Many dogs, Australian Shepherds included, get into trouble at home and in the yard because they do not get enough exercise. Teaching your dog to retrieve is a wonderful way to make sure it gets regular daily exercise and, as an added attraction, interaction with you.

Many Aussies are natural retrievers, which means they will naturally chase anything you throw, then bring the item back to you. Others may not have the instinctive drive to retrieve and need to learn the skills involved. If you approach this as you would any training challenge you can teach your Aussie to retrieve.

Make a game out of retrieving rather than a chore or work. If you think of it as a game, your dog will pick that up, making the retrieve much more attractive to learn. To begin, teach the retrieve by using a toy that you know your dog likes and save it for these training sessions. Do not give it to the dog at any other time.

Show the dog the toy and encourage the dog to grab it. When it does, play a little tug of war. "Fetch it, yeah! Good dog!" Take the toy away from your dog, gently telling the dog "Give" and toss the toy a couple of feet away. Encourage the dog to grab it. "Fetch it!" If your dog does not immediately go for it, grab it yourself and play "keep away." Get the dog excited, even tease the dog with it. When your dog does grab it, praise it. Repeat this three or four times and stop the training session. You want to stop while your dog is still excited.

Repeat the entire game a couple hours later. If your Aussie is catching on and is starting to grab for the toy, throw it just a little farther the next time, four feet away instead of two feet away. Gradually increase the distance but continue running after the toy yourself so that you can grab it if your dog does not. "Keep away" games can be exciting to your dog and that excitement is important right now.

When your dog is enthusiastically chasing the toy and picking it up, stop running after it and instead verbally encourage your dog to bring the toy back to you. "Bring it here, come! Good dog!" If your dog hesitates, back away from it, even turn and run away. Praise your dog when it brings the toy to you.

Once your dog has the idea of the retrieve and is reliably chasing after and bringing back its favorite toy, start using other toys. Throw a tennis ball, a soccer ball, a Frisbee, even a boomerang. Use the same commands and teach it the same way.

Solving Problems

Many problems are the result of allowing your Aussie, as a puppy, to get away with things that you find you do not like when it has grown up. It might be cute when your dog nips your heels as a ten-week-old puppy, but it is annoying and hurts when a ten-month-old dog does it. Do not allow your Aussie to do anything as a puppy that you are not going to want it to do when it is full grown.

Many other behavior problems are the result of too little exercise, not enough training and a lack of family or pack

Ch. Brookridge Syl Ver Bull It CDX, TT

"Bullet"

OWNERS: SHARON AND JOE WILLIS
BREEDER: SUSAN MOOREHEAD

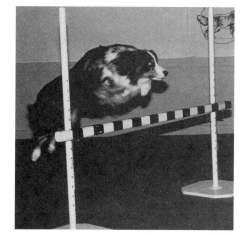

Sharon relays Bullet's story, "About a year after I got Bullet, we went to bed at the usual time. Just as I was drifting off to sleep, Bullet started jumping on top of me, acting totally obnoxious, which is very unusual for him. I finally decided that something was wrong and I got up to let him outside; as I started downstairs I smelled smoke, then heard the smoke detector go off."

"Continuing downstairs, I saw that the toaster oven was smoking. I had left a newspaper on top of it and because of faulty wiring, the toaster came on and was scorching the paper. It was just about ready to burst into flames. Thanks to Bullet, there was no other damage."

At six years old, Bullet continues to excel in both breed and obedience competition. In conformation, besides winning his numerous championships, he has been the Top Champion in Georgia for the last three years. In obedience, Bullet has qualified and competed in Gaines/Cycle competitions and is presently training in utility.

Sharon continued, "They say a great dog comes along but once in a lifetime; well, Bullet is my great dog. He has numerous accomplishments but what he does best is be my loving companion."

leadership. Other problems can result from boredom, environmental stress, personality or physical problems or nutritional deficiencies.

It is important to try and figure out why a dog has a problem rather than simply treating the symptoms. However, to discover the cause, you may need to think like a detective. Ask your neighbors when your Aussie started barking; was it after another neighbor started remodeling? Perhaps the noise of the power tools is bothering it. Or did your dog start barking after a neighbor

adopted a new dog? When did your dog start chewing on the picnic table? Was it after you switched dog foods?

You may also need to take your Aussie to the veterinarian before you figure out the cause of the problem behavior. A urinary tract infection can cause a dog to "forget" its housetraining. Thyroid problems can masquerade as behavior problems. An ear infection, tooth abscess or impacted anal glands can all cause behavior problems.

By putting together pieces of the puzzle you can try to figure out the cause of the problem. Then you can treat the cause as well as correct the problem and prevent it from happening again. Almost all behavior problems can be approached using the same basic formula: 1. Treat the cause of the problem when possible. 2. Prevent the problem from occurring. 3. Teach or correct your Aussie when you catch it in the act.

JUMPING ON PEOPLE

Dogs greet each other face-to-face, especially when a submissive dog meets a more dominant dog. The submissive dog will lick the face or mouth of the dominant one. Your dog jumps on you for the same reason; it wants to lick your face and does not understand why you do not like it.

You can give your Aussie the attention it needs and teach it not to jump on you by emphasizing the sit. When your dog sits in front of you while you pet it, it is getting the attention from you that it craves. Your dog can not sit, hold still for petting and jump on you at the same time. It is impossible.

CHEWING AND HOUSEHOLD DESTRUCTION

Dogs chew for a variety of reasons; they chew when they are teething, bored, hungry or when they have too much energy. Unfortunately, chewing can lead to health problems if the dog ingests something that it should not and it can also be very expensive. It is much cheaper to give the dog a two dollar leather rawhide to chew than it is to let it chew up your two hundred dollar leather shoes.

Prevention is the most important key to controlling household destruction. Do not let your dog (especially when it is a puppy) have free run of the house if you can not watch it. Close closet doors and keep dirty laundry, shoes, gloves and slippers put away. Put up baby gates so that your Aussie can not sneak into a back bedroom to steal something. Puppy-proof your house, picking up and putting away anything that you do not want your dog to bother.

When you are home and able to supervise your Aussie, you can teach it what is allowed and what is not. Earlier in this chapter, we discussed how to use a squirt bottle as an interruption; you can use it to teach your Aussie to drop anything you did not want it to pick up. If your Aussie comes trotting down the hall with a slipper in its mouth, squirt the dog as you say, "Drop it!" When your dog drops it, take it away and hand it one of its toys. "Here! This is yours, play with this. Good dog!" You are correcting what is wrong and then showing it what is right.

The squirt bottle, filled with water and a touch of vinegar, works because your dog's most important sense is its sense of smell and the vinegar water smells bad. Your dog stops whatever it is doing to lick the bad-smelling stuff off its nose, or to rub it off and at that time you can praise it for stopping whatever was wrong. Again, you are then not simply interrupting or correcting what was wrong, but most importantly, you are also showing the dog what is right.

Digging and other destructive behaviors are usually the result of boredom. Remember to give your Aussie a "job" of its own.

DIGGING

A digging dog can be just as destructive as a chewing dog, if not more so. A backyard dug up by an enthusiastic dog can look as though a herd of gophers were rampaging through it. Some breeds are more prone to digging than others; for example, terriers can be awful. Luckily, Australian Shepherds are not prone to digging, although they are certainly capable if there was some motivation for it, such as a trespassing gopher.

Digging can be discouraged by picking up the dog's feces and burying them back into the hole that your dog dug, covering the feces with dirt. Your dog will go back to that hole, take one sniff and leave it alone. Digging under a fence can be prevented by nailing some hardware cloth or chicken wire to the bottom of the fence, bending it under so that it extends into the yard.

If you can catch your Aussie in the act of digging, correct your dog for it: "Shame! Bad dog! Look what you did!" Unfortunately, catching most dogs in the act is difficult.

BARKING

Dogs bark for many reasons, just as people vocalize and talk for a number of different reasons. They bark when they are bored, when someone walks by the yard, when they want attention or when they want to play. Some dogs, like people, are more vocal than others. Some bark, some whine, some howl and some even seem like they are trying to talk. Although Aussies are not normally problem barkers, many Aussies do like to vocalize and they do need to be taught to stop barking on a command.

As we have said before, the squirt bottle is a very effective way to interrupt behavior, including barking. When your dog is at the front door, barking, squirt and at the same time, tell the dog, "Quiet!" When your dog stops barking to lick its nose, say "Good dog to be quiet!"

Training Is an Ongoing Process

Training your Aussie is an on-going process that does not stop. Just as you continue to learn throughout your life, so should your dog. A brain that is not used becomes stagnant.

Keep working on these basic commands until your dog is proficient, then start teaching new things.

Trick training is a lot of fun, is great for entertaining guests and can be challenging. Tricks such as shake hands, roll over, sneeze and walk on the back legs are great. Play dead is one of my favorites and I have had a lot of fun with it. One day I was talking to a friend who happens to be a police officer. I knew he had a good sense of humor and I decided to have some fun with him. So I turned to my dog, that was sitting by my side and I asked him, "Care Bear,

Ch. Showtime's Surprise CD. The intelligent Australian Shepherd is a joy to train and can be taught many tricks.

would you rather be a cop or a dead dog?" I emphasized the words "dead dog," as they are Bear's cue. Upon hearing them, he dropped down, stretched out on the ground, flat on his side and looked dead. I started laughing, my friend went bugged-eyed, hesitated, then started laughing so hard tears were running down his cheeks and Bear got up, barking. It was great fun and my friend has told many people about it, requiring Bear and I to show off again and again.

There are also a number of different dog sports that you and your Aussie can become involved with that will challenge both of you. The fact that your Aussie will be more interested in the amount of time you spend with it than how you spend that time is a positive indication of the nature of this wonderful breed. So you pick the sport, any sport, and have fun.

CHAPTER 5

Conformation Competition

DOG SHOWS have been around a long time. The first conformation show, of which records still exist, was held in 1859 at Newcastle-on-Tyne, England. They became part of American life in the 1870s and the first Westminster Kennel Club Show was held in New York in May, 1877. This show, the most prestigious in the United States, is the second oldest continuously held sporting event in America. (The oldest is the Kentucky Derby horse race.)

Conformation competition is, as the name implies, competition in which a judge evaluates the way your Aussie's body is formed and put together, its gait, movement and showmanship. Each dog is judged against, or compared to, a written standard or set of guidelines which state how a dog of each breed should look and move. This standard is used to measure each dog's qualities and faults against the other dogs of that breed competing on a particular day.

Every breed recognized by a dog show registry, such as the Australian Shepherd Club of America, the American Kennel Club and the United Kennel Club, has a breed standard. The standard describes each individual characteristic of the breed and is what keeps an Australian Shepherd looking like an Australian Shepherd instead of a Collie or a Greyhound.

At any given dog show there can be entries up to two or three thousand dogs or even more. The people attending will include novices at their first show with a beloved family pet, seasoned veterans with their fourth or fifth generation dogs, professional handlers driving recreational vehicles carrying many dogs, even venders selling everything from dog food to handmade refrigerator magnets. The American Kennel Club, in The AKC's World of the Purebred Dog, describes the modern dog show as "a blend of circus, fashion show, barber shop, beauty pageant, gambling casino, class reunion, political caucus and picnic."

All social activities aside, the primary purpose of the conformation competition dog show is to preserve each breed by selecting the best representatives of the standard from the dogs competing each day. The person

Ch. Arrogance of Heatherhill CD, STDd and ASCA Hall of Fame Sire.

who is judging the dogs has studied the breed standard, apprenticed under a senior judge and then has been tested as to his or her knowledge of the breed. However, each judge's interpretation of the written standard can be slightly different and a dog that wins one day under one judge may lose the next day under another judge. That is simply part of the sport. However, a dog that wins consistently under several different judges and against other dogs in competition is generally considered to be a good representative of its breed and therefore worthy of being bred and passing on its characteristics and breed traits.

This dog will, as it wins, earn its championship (Ch.), which will then be listed on its registration papers and the pedigree for its offspring.

The American Kennel Club states that to be called a champion a dog must "Earn fifteen points, under at least three different judges, and of those fifteen points, at least two wins must be of major points." The number of points awarded for a win varies from region to region across the country and varies from breed to breed, and even varies according to the sex of the dogs competing. The point schedule will also change yearly, depending upon the number of dogs and bitches competing.

In the registries of other countries, the title of champion is not quite so simplistic. In Great Britain, a Labrador Retriever (and many other breeds) must earn a working certificate before it can be awarded a conformation championship. Germany has similar requirements; most working breeds must first compete in working trials. In Mexico, depending upon the breed, many dogs must first pass a temperament test or working test.

Because the AKC's definition of a champion does not take into account the working characteristics that are vitally important to many breeds, including the Australian Shepherd, many breed clubs have instituted programs to encourage working the dog in obedience and in its traditional functions. The Newfoundland Club of America has active Water Rescue and Draft Dog Programs, the Dalmatian Club of America has a coach dog program and other breed clubs emphasize herding, tracking, schutzhund and other activities relating to the breed's working or herding heritage.

The Australian Shepherd Club of America has long maintained an emphasis on the Aussie's working and herding heritage and offers Versatility Champion title and a Supreme Versatility Champion titles, which incorporate the conformation championship with obedience and stockdog titles.

The definition of what "champion" means is difficult. The American Kennel Club has one definition, as do the other registries that recognize Australian Shepherds. Serious fanciers of the breed have a definition of champion, and so does the average dog owner. Unfortunately, all of these definitions are not the same. To some people, "champion" means a dog has satisfied the conformation competition requirements, while to other

Int. Mex./Am. ASCA Canadian and States Kennel Club Ch. Bayshore's Three To Get Ready CD, TT, STDd and ASCA Hall of Fame Sire.

people it means strength of character or heroic behavior. To others it may mean the ability to pass on traits to its offspring, or it may simply be a red "Ch." on a pedigree.

There are some definitions that "champion" does not fit; it does not mean the dog is free of hereditary defects, such as hip dysplasia or PRA. It is no guarantee of a reliable temperament or a good personality, nor does it guarantee the dog is intelligent or trainable. "Champion" does not mean the dog is capable of passing on its good traits; in fact, many popular breed champions have not been able to reproduce themselves successfully.

Because the word "champion" has so many definitions, to clarify matters, in this chapter we will be referring to a conformation champion as defined by the American Kennel Club and the Australian Shepherd Club of America.

Ch. County Hotline of Agua Dulce CDX with Jr. Handler Tiffany Levin.

Competing in Conformation

All competition starts in what is known as the breed competition or the breed ring. All dogs compete against members of their own breed, with the classes divided by sex; bitches compete against other bitches and dogs against other dogs. Dogs of either sex that have not earned their championship are called "class" dogs and can compete in a number of different classes. Puppy classes are available for puppies between six and nine months, nine to twelve months and twelve to eighteen months.

The Novice class is available for dogs over six months of age that have not previously won three first places in the Novice class or have not won a first place in any other class, nor have won any points

toward their championship. The Bred by Exhibitor class is self explanatory; the dog must be owned and shown by its breeder. The American Bred class is for dogs bred and whelped in the United States. The Open class is for any dog over six months of age that is not a champion and in Australian Shepherds, as with a few other breeds, the Open class is divided by color. There is an Open class for blacks, blue merles, reds and red merles.

Each dog competes in only one class, with the dogs (males) competing first. When the steward (judge's helper) calls the class, the competitors will usually go into the ring in catalog order (arm band order). The judge will explain to the class what he wishes the competitors to do, such as the ring pattern for gaiting, and so on. At the completion of judging for each class, the judge will award ribbons to the winners and then dismiss the class. When all of the classes for dogs (males) have been completed, all of the class first

Ch. Mistretta's Gabriella Maja ATDd, STDsc.

place winners will go back into the ring for the selection of the Winners Dog (WD), or the judge's choice for the best non-champion male dog that day. The Winners Dog is awarded points toward its championship based on the number of dogs competing in the classes, as discussed earlier.

When the dogs' classes are completed, the bitches' classes compete in the same manner. A Winners Bitch (WB) is selected from the winners of all the classes and she is awarded points towards her championship based on the number of bitches defeated.

When the Winners Dog and Winners Bitch have been decided, they return to the ring with all of the champion dogs and bitches (called "specials") that are entered in the Best of Breed (BOB) competition. The judge will choose Best of Breed, then will choose a Best of Winners (BOW) from between the Winners Dog and Winners Bitch. The next decision will be to choose the Best of Opposite Sex (BOS). If the judge chooses a dog Best of Breed, the

Ch. Propwash Ghostrider USASA National Specialty Winners Dog, 1993 pictured at six months.

Best of Opposite will be a bitch, and visa versa. (If you are confused, Appendix C is an outline of how the judging proceeds.)

At this point the competition is over for all of the dogs competing in the breed class except for the dog or bitch chosen as Best of Breed. The winning Aussie in AKC competition still has more work ahead. When all of the breed judging is completed for all of the breeds, the group judging starts. Australian Shepherds are in the Herding Group. All of the Best of Breed winners from the Herding Group will go back to the ring for a Group Judge to determine which BOB winner best represents it's standard for first place in the group. The winner of the group will then compete with the other group winners for the Best in Show (BIS) competition. Obviously, winning Best in Show is a tremendous thrill.

Ch. Sweet Season's of Heatherhill, ASCA National Specialty Winners Bitch, 1975.

Ch. Brigadoon's One Arrogant Dude, ASCA Hall of Fame Sire and ASCA National Specialty Winners Dog and Best of Winners, 1985.

Preparation

To compete well in conformation, a show dog must be a good representative of its breed. However, it takes more to make a champion. If you decide you want to enter your Aussie in a few shows, either for its championship or just to see how your dog would do, there is some work you need to do first.

Your Aussie will need some training; it will need to trot on a loose leash, moving out smoothly and quickly without weaving all over, bumping into you or jumping on you. It will also need to know how to stack, or stand four-square, with a foot under each corner of its body. Your Aussie will need to learn to let a stranger touch its body; the judge will run his hands all over your dog, checking body structure, teeth and, with the male dogs making certain they have two descended testicles. Training your Aussie prior to the show will allow you and your dog to gain confidence in what you are doing so when you do compete, you will look better in the ring.

That confidence is part of what makes up showmanship, another part of competition. Many times the dog that wins is the one that, as the experts say, "Asks for the win." It is hard to say exactly what that is. Sometimes its the way a dog carries itself, sometimes it's the look in the dog's eyes, or the way it stacks itself. Many times it's an extra sparkle, an attitude that says to the judge, "Hey, look at me!"

You also need to learn how to show your Aussie so your dog can look its best. Handling is a skill and if you have never done it before, show handling classes can help both you and your Aussie gain confidence, showmanship and learn the ring routine. Ask your local dog trainer if she has conformation classes or can recommend you to one. Or ask your local kennel club or Aussie club for a referral to a good class.

Your Aussie must be in good physical condition for the shows. A competition dog should be firm and muscular without too much fat padding the ribs. Keep in mind the Australian Shepherd is a herding dog and your Aussie's fitness level should show it is capable of doing the job. Good physical fitness will also be reflected in the dog's bright eyes, shiny coat, the way the dog carries itself and its overall bearing. Showing can be stressful and good physical fitness will help your dog stand up to the physical and emotional stresses of showing.

Your Aussie must be well groomed for the show. If your dog has been chewing because of some allergies or fleas or its coat is out of condition, do not show it until the coat has grown back. Bathe and brush the dog prior to the show day. Check to make sure its ears are clean and healthy, its teeth are clean and there is no matter in its eyes. Check for fleas and ticks, burrs and foxtails. Trim up the loose hair around its feet and trim the excess hair between the pads but do not go overboard with the scissors; Australian Shepherds should be shown looking natural. Bring a comb to the show so you can comb out your dog's coat just before you go in the ring.

You must also be well groomed for the show. It is not necessary to look like Miss America or Mr. Universe, but you should be well groomed, neat and clean. Most professional women handlers wear a dress or skirt, preferably something with pockets where you can hide liver treats and a comb. Male professional handlers wear a suit or nice slacks and a sports jacket, again with pockets. No matter what you wear, make sure you can move comfortably, both to bend over your Aussie and to run with it in the ring. Comfortable shoes are also a necessity.

Entering a Show

The American Kennel Club (AKC) licenses or sanctions clubs to hold all-breed and single-breed specialty shows. All recognized breeds (including the Australian Shepherd) can be shown in conformation classes, to earn championship points, at an AKC all breed show. A specialty show is held by a single-breed club, and can be held by an AKC-recognized national club or a regional club, and competition is limited to a single breed. The Australian Shepherd Club of America holds specialty shows for Australian Shepherds only, as well as all breed obedience trials.

Matches are practices for shows. Run in a similar manner to shows, matches are usually more relaxed, and no points are

At a dog show the judge will examine your dog's bite or ask you to show the bite.

awarded to winners. Matches can be good practice for you to learn how to show your Aussie and for your dog to get some ring experience, get used to being judged and to become familiar with the show environment.

Matches can usually be entered on the day of the match, but most shows require you to pre-enter, often several weeks prior to the event. When you find out about a show you would like to enter, get a copy of the premium list (a flyer which lists all the details of the show) including where it is being held, the date, time, classes offered and an entry blank. (See Appendix B) Send your completed entry

Ch. My Main Man of Heatherhill, Best of Breed at the USASA National Specialty, 1994 and Best of Opposite Sex at the ASCA National Specialty, 1992.

form to the address listed, with your check for the entry fee. About a week prior to the show you will receive confirmation of your entry with the time you will be competing, the ring number and your armband number.

You can find out about shows and matches through your local Australian Shepherd club or local dog training club. Local trainers, groomers, veterinarians or pet stores personnel may also be helpful. In addition, the AKC and ASCA both publish upcoming events in their club publications.

Grooming for a dog show requires time and skill.

Mistretta's Rough Eagle STDdsc.

Show Etiquette

As with any sport, there are some written and unwritten rules all competitors should follow. First of all, write to the registries you plan to compete under for a copy of their rules and regulations applying to dog shows. (See Appendix A)

When you arrive at a show, buy a catalog. You can usually find it at the show officials' table. This book will list all the dogs competing, by breed and class. You can then confirm when your breed judging is, what ring it is in and what dogs are ahead of you. Check into your ring by letting the ring steward know you are there, giving him your armband number, and picking up your armband which you will wear on your left arm. Watch the classes ahead of you and be ready to go into the ring when it is your turn. Do not be late. Watching the classes before you will also let you see the judge's ring procedures so you will know what to expect when it is your turn.

When the winners are announced in your class, be a gracious winner if you have won, thanking the judge. If you have not won, be a gracious loser and congratulate the winner. Never, ever stomp out, muttering about the dogs that won or the quality of the judging. Be a good sport.

Before and after your judging, watch your dog. Do not let it interfere with other dogs, even to sniff. Keep your dog close to you. If yours has an accident, pick it up before someone steps in it. Be considerate of your fellow competitors and the grounds committee that will have to clean up the mess.

The Australian Shepherd Standards

As was mentioned previously in this chapter, the breed standard is the guideline which states exactly what an Australian Shepherd should be. This blueprint is what guides breeders trying to produce better dogs. Judges looking at the dogs exhibited before them at a show can compare them to the ideal dog as described in the standard. The standard is the most important tool available to anyone concerned with the Australian Shepherd today and in the future.

The breed standard that exists today was not written casually. In 1975, the Australian Shepherd Club of America formed a committee to formalize a standard. This committee,

headed by Robert Kline, D.V.M., was made up of some of the breed's prominent breeders, veterinarians, judges and stockmen. Input was accepted from the membership, affiliate clubs, breeders and experts on canine structure and gait. The finalized standard was accepted in November, 1975. A revision was requested by the ASCA membership, gained unanimous approval and the present standard became effective in January, 1977.

When the American Kennel Club recognized the breed, the standard accepted by the AKC contained a few changes from the standard recognized by ASCA. Therefore, at this writing, there are two standards for the Australian Shepherd, one for ASCA and one for the AKC.

The following are the complete standards of each organization, illustrating some of what both have as a vision of the ideal Australian Shepherd. Also included are some comments explaining terms and comparing some of the similarities and differences between the two standards.

Australian Shepherd Club of America, Inc.
(Effective January 15, 1977)

American Kennel Club
(Effective January 1, 1993)

GENERAL APPEARANCE

(ASCA) The Australian Shepherd is a well-balanced dog of medium size and bone. He is attentive and animated, showing strength and stamina combined with unusual agility. Slightly longer than tall, he has a coat of moderate length and coarseness with coloring that offers variety and individuality in each specimen. An identifying characteristic is his natural or docked bobtail. In each sex, masculinity or femininity is well-defined.

(AKC) The Australian Shepherd is an intelligent working dog of strong herding and guarding instincts. He is a loyal companion and has the stamina to work all day. He is well balanced, slightly longer than tall of medium size and bone, with coloring that offers variety and individuality. He is attentive and animated, lithe and agile, solid and muscular without cloddiness. He has a coat of moderate length and coarseness. He has a docked or natural bobbed tail.

(These introductory paragraphs set the stage for the rest of the standards. We are

Ch. Tri-Ivory Roquefort of Higgins CD, Best of Breed at the ASCA National Specialties in 1985 and 1988, and ASCA Hall of Fame Sire, in 1984.

looking for a well-proportioned dog of medium size that is capable of working hard, an athlete. There are obvious similarities in both introductory paragraphs; the dogs are described as medium-sized, longer than tall and so on. One difference is the ASCA description specifically mentions a difference between males and females, the AKC does not.)

CHARACTER

(ASCA) The Australian Shepherd is intelligent, primarily a working dog of strong herding and guardian instincts. He is an exceptional companion. He is versatile and easily trained, performing his assigned tasks with great style and enthusiasm. He is reserved with strangers but does not exhibit shyness. Although an aggressive, authoritative worker, viciousness towards people or animals is intolerable.

TEMPERAMENT

(AKC) The Australian Shepherd is an intelligent, active dog with an even disposition, he is good natured, seldom quarrelsome. They may be somewhat reserved in initial meetings. Faults: Any display of shyness, fear or aggression is to be severely penalized.

(The AKC standard mentioned character or temperament in the general appearance paragraph so this paragraph is somewhat shorter. The ASCA description commented more on the dog's working abilities. Both mentioned the dog should not be shy, fearful or aggressive towards people; although the language is different.)

HEAD

(ASCA) Clean-cut, strong, dry and in proportion to the body. The top-skull is flat to slightly rounded, its length and width each equal to the length of the muzzle which is in balance and proportioned to the rest of the head. The muzzle tapers slightly to a rounded tip. The stop is moderate but well defined.

Head types may differ—no one type more correct than another. Note the differences in the three heads illustrated in this section. All conform to the breed standard.

(AKC) The head is clean cut, strong and dry. Overall size should be in proportion to the body. The muzzle is equal in length or slightly shorter than the back skull. Viewed from the side, the topline of the back skull and muzzle form parallel planes, divided by a moderate, well defined stop. The muzzle tapers little from base to nose and is rounded at the tip.

(There are two slightly different pictures here. ASCA wants a top-skull "Flat to slightly rounded," whereas AKC sees "The topline of the backskull and muzzle form parallel planes".)

EXPRESSION

(AKC) Showing attentiveness and intelligence, alert and eager. Gaze should be keen but friendly.

EYES

(ASCA) Very expressive, showing attentiveness and intelligence. Clear, almond-shaped, and of moderate size, set a little obliquely, neither prominent nor sunken, with pupils dark, well-defined and perfectly positioned. Color is brown, blue, amber or any variation or combination, including flecks and marbling.

(AKC) Expression should show attentiveness and intelligence, alert and eager. Gaze should be keen but friendly. Eyes are brown, blue, amber or any variation or combination thereof, including flecks or marbling. Almond shaped, not protruding nor sunken. The blue merles and blacks have black pigmentation on eye rims. The reds and red merles have liver (brown) pigmentation on eye rims.

(A notable difference between these two paragraphs is the mention of the oblique eye set of the Australian Shepherd mentioned in the ASCA standard but not mentioned at all in the AKC standard. An oblique eye set is said to be dependent upon the zygomatic arch. The flatter the arch (lesser degree of curvature) the more oblique the eye set. When the curve of the arch is more prominent, the eyes will be set more towards the front of the head. The moderate arch mentioned in the ASCA standard calls for enough arch for good front and side vision but a flat enough arch for protection from dangers associated with the breed's natural work: bushes, brambles and the debris thrown up by flying hooves. The ASCA standard also calls for perfectly positioned pupils. Unfortunately, the breed has been known to have some eye defects and an off-set pupil is an easily seen defect that may be a clue to other underlying problems.)

TEETH

(ASCA) A full compliment of strong, white teeth meet in a scissors bite. An even bite is a fault. Teeth broken or missing by accident are not penalized. Disqualifications: Undershot bites; overshot bites exceeding 1/8 inch.

(AKC) A full compliment of strong white teeth should meet in a scissors bite or may meet in a level bite. Disqualifications: Undershot; overshot by greater than 1/8 inch. Loss of contact caused by short center incisors in an otherwise correct bite shall not be judged undershot. Teeth missing or broken by accident shall not be penalized.

(When the AKC standard was adopted many people were concerned with the acceptance of an even bite. Most canine bite experts feel a scissors bite is indicative of a proper jaw assembly and the scissors bite allows a herding dog to correctly "grip" livestock with a pinching motion instead of a puncturing bite which could damage livestock. A female dog without the proper scissors bite might not be able to correctly sever the umbilical cords of her puppies. Although the ASCA standard does not disqualify an even bite, it is a fault, as breed experts felt that teeth in a jaw with an even bite were more prone to wear by the constant meeting of the teeth and more likely to be injured or broken.)

EARS

(ASCA) Set on high at the side of the head, triangular and slightly rounded at the tip, of moderate size with the length measured by bringing the tip of the ear around to the inside corner of the eye. The ears, at full attention, break slightly forward and over from one-quarter to one-half above the base. Prick ears and hound-type ears are severe faults.

(AKC) Ears are triangular of moderate size and leather, set high at the head. At full attention they break forward and over, or to the side as a rose ear. Prick ears and hanging ears are severe faults.

MUZZLE

(AKC) Muzzle tapers little from base to nose and is rounded at the tip.

NOSE

(AKC) Blue merles and blacks have black pigmentation on the nose (and lips). Red merles and reds have liver (brown) pigmentation on the

An example of a correct Australian Shepherd profile.

nose (and lips). On the merles it is permissible to have small pink spots, however, they should not exceed 25% of the nose on dogs over one year of age; which is a serious fault.

NECK AND BODY

(ASCA) The neck is firm, clean and in proportion to the body. It is of medium length and slightly arched at the crest, setting well into the shoulders. The body is firm and muscular. The topline appears level at a natural four-square stance. The chest is deep and strong with ribs well-sprung. The loin is strong and broad when viewed

Correct front structure.

from the top. The bottom line carries well back with a moderate tuck-up. The croup is moderately sloping, the ideal being thirty (30) degrees from the horizontal. The tail is straight, not to exceed four (4) inches, natural bobtail or docked.

(AKC) Neck is strong, of moderate length slightly arched at the crest, fitting well into the shoulders.

Topline. Back is straight and strong, level and firm from withers to hip joints. The croup is moderately sloped.

Chest is not broad but is deep with the lowest point reaching the elbow. The ribs are well sprung and long, neither barrel chested nor slab-sided. The underline shows a moderate tuck-up.

Tail is straight, docked or naturally bobbed, not to exceed four inches in length.

FOREQUARTERS

(ASCA) The shoulder blades (scapula) are long and flat, close set at the withers, approximately two fingers width at a natural stance and well laid back at an angle approximating forty-five (45) degrees to the ground. The upper arm (humerus) is attached at an approximate right angle to the shoulder line with fore legs dropping straight, perpendicular to the ground. The elbow joint is equidistant from the ground to the withers. The legs are straight and powerful. Pasterns are short, thick and strong but still flexible, showing a slight angle when viewed from the side. Feet are oval shaped, compact, with close-knit, well-arched toes. Pads are thick and resilient; nails short and strong. Dewclaws may be removed.

HINDQUARTERS

(ASCA) Width of hindquarters approximately equal to the width of the forequarters at the shoulders. The angulation of the pelvis and upper thigh (femur) corresponds to the angulation of the shoulder blade and upper arm forming an approximate right angle. Stifles are clearly defined, hock joints moderately bent. The metatarsi are short, perpendicular to the ground and parallel to each other when viewed from the rear. Feet are oval shaped, compact, with close-knit, well-arched toes. Pads are thick and resilient; nails short and strong. Rear dewclaws are removed.

(AKC) The width of the hindquarters is equal to the width of the forequarters at the shoulders. The angulation of the pelvis and upper thigh corresponds to the angulation of the shoulder blade and upper arm, forming an approximate right

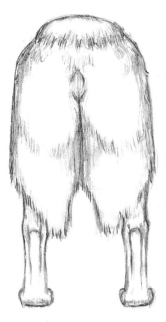

Correct rear structure.

(AKC) Shoulder blades are long, flat, fairly close set at the withers and well laid back. The upper arm, which should be relatively the same length as the shoulder blade, attaches at an approximate right angle to the shoulder line with forelegs dropping straight, on a perpendicular to the ground.

Legs. Legs are straight and strong. Bone is strong, oval rather than round. Pastern is medium length and very slightly sloped. Front dew claws may be removed.

Feet are oval, compact with close knit, well arched toes. Pads are thick and resilient.

Cloverhill Propwash Bustle, Black-Tri.

Red-Tri

Moonlights Ruler of the Roost, Red Merle.

Ch. Starswept's Out of the Blue, Blue Merle.

angle. Stifles are clearly defined, hock joints moderately bent. The hocks are short, perpendicular to the ground and parallel to each other when viewed from the rear. Rear dew claws must be removed.

Feet are oval, compact with close knit, well arched toes. Pads are thick and resilient.

COAT

(ASCA) Of medium texture, straight to slightly wavy, weather resistant, of moderate length with an undercoat. The quantity of coat varies with climate. Hair is short and smooth on the head, outside of ears, front of forelegs and below the hocks. Backs of forelegs are moderately feathered; breeches are moderately full. There is a moderate mane and frill, more pronounced in dogs than in bitches. Non-typical coats are severe faults.

(AKC) Hair is of medium texture, straight to wavy, weather resistant and of medium length. The undercoat varies in quantity with variations in climate. Hair is short and smooth on the head, ears, front of forelegs and below the hocks. Backs of forelegs and britches are moderately feathered. There is a moderate mane and frill, more pronounced in dogs than in bitches. Non-typical coats are severe faults.

COLOR

(ASCA) All colors are strong, clear and rich. The recognized colors are blue merle, red (liver) merle, solid black and solid red (liver) all with or without white marking and/or tan (copper) points with no reference. The blue merle and black have black pigmentation on the nose, lips and eye rims; the red (liver) and red (liver) merle have liver pigmentation on nose, lips and eye rims. Butterfly nose should not be faulted under one year of age. On all colors, the areas surrounding the ears and eyes are dominated by color other than white. The hairline of a white collar does not exceed the point of the withers. Disqualifications: Other than recognized colors. White body splashes. Dudley nose.

(AKC) Blue merle, black, red merle, red - all with or without white marking and/or tan (copper) points, with no order of preference. The hairline of a white collar does not exceed the point of the withers at the skin. White is acceptable on the neck (either in part or as a full collar) chest, legs, muzzle underparts, blaze on head and white extension from underpart up to four inches measuring from a horizontal line at the elbow. White on the head should not predominate and the eyes must be fully surrounded by color and pigment. Merles characteristically become darker with increasing age. Disqualifications: White body splashes, which means white on the body between withers and tail, on the sides between elbows and the back of hindquarters on all colors.

(Both of these descriptions are similar, although the AKC standard offers more detail regarding white markings. The ASCA standard mentioned "rich" colors and also mentioned the disqualification of a butterfly or dudley nose. A butterfly nose is a nose than has incomplete pigmentation. In most puppies the color will fill in rapidly and almost all will be filled in prior to one year of age. However, a dudley nose, or a nose without pigmentation is a disqualification; the unpigmented nose is susceptible to sunburn, dermatitis due to repeated sunburns, even skin cancer.)

GAIT

(ASCA) Smooth, free and easy; exhibiting agility of movement with a well-balanced, ground-covering stride. Fore and rear legs move straight and parallel with the center line of the body; as speed increases, the feet, both front and rear, converge toward the center line of gravity of the dog, while the topline remains firm and level.

(AKC) The Australian Shepherd has a smooth, free and easy gait. He exhibits great agility of movement with a well-balanced, ground covering stride. Fore and hind legs move straight and parallel with the center line of the body. As speed increases, the feet, front and rear, converge toward the center line of gravity of the dog while the back remains firm and level. The Australian Shepherd must be agile and able to change direction or alter gait instantly.

An example of the free flowing movement for which the Australian Shepherd is known.

Ch. Winchester's Hotline, ASCA Hall of Fame Sire.

SIZE

(ASCA) Preferred height at the withers for males is 20 to 23 inches; that for females is 18 to 21 inches, however, quality is not to be sacrificed in favor of size.

(AKC) The preferred height for males is 20-23 inches and females 18-21 inches. Quality is not to be sacrificed in favor of size.

PROPORTION

(AKC) Measuring from the breastbone to the rear of the thigh and from the top of the withers to the ground, the Australian Shepherd is slightly longer than tall.

SUBSTANCE

(AKC) Solidly built with moderate bone. Structure in the male reflects masculinity without coarseness. Bitches appear feminine without being slight of bone.

DISQUALIFICATIONS

(ASCA) Monorchidism and cryptorchidism.

(AKC) Undershot. Overshot greater than 1/8 inch. White body splashes, which means white on the body between withers and tail, on sides between elbows and back of hindquarters in all colors.

If you are having trouble understanding the words of the standard and their application to real dogs, try reading the standard with your Aussie in front of you. If you still have questions, do not be afraid to ask. Go to a show and ask a couple of different people how they interpret the standard and ask them to demonstrate on a dog. Also, after the completion of competition, many judges will be happy to express an opinion about your dog. The different viewpoints expressed by a variety of people will either clarify the standard for you, or totally confuse you. Australian Shepherd clubs often host seminars, asking judges and breeders to speak on different subjects, including interpreting the standard. Ask your local club if anything is planned for the near future.

CHAPTER 6

Obedience Competition

OBEDIENCE COMPETITION is an opportunity for dog owners to demonstrate the teamwork they have developed with their dogs. Competition requires the dog and owner to master certain exercises which vary depending upon the class entered. In addition, all dogs competing must be well socialized to other people and dogs and able to concentrate in different locations and circumstances. To compete successfully, an owner and his or her dog must have a sound relationship based on mutual trust, respect, good communication skills and a sense of fun.

The American Kennel Club regulations state: "The purpose of Obedience Trials is to demonstrate the usefulness of the pure-bred dog as a companion of man, not merely the dog's ability to follow specified routines in the obedience ring ... the basic objective of obedience trials is to produce dogs that have been trained and conditioned to behave in the home, in public places, and in the presence of other dogs, in a manner that will reflect credit on the sport of obedience."

The Australian Shepherd Club of America has a similar introduction to its obedience regulations and prefaces it with this statement, "Obedience Trials are a sport and all participants should be guided by the principles of good sportsmanship both in and outside the ring."

Taycin's Blu Angel of Arovista UD, ATDds; the fifteenth ASCA UD of record and dam of Lawson's Cool Shamus, UD, ATDds.

In obedience competition, dogs and owners compete in different classes to earn obedience titles. Whereas conformation competition awards only one title, "Champion," obedience offers several. Australian Shepherds can compete and earn obedience titles with three different registries. The Australian Shepherd Club of America (ASCA) offers Companion Dog (CD), Companion Dog Excellent (CDX), Utility Dog (UD) and Obedience Trial Champion (OTCH). The American Kennel Club offers the same titles, plus the Utility Dog Excellent (UDX) and the United Kennel Club offers similar titles, Companion Dog (U-CD), Companion Dog Excellent (U-CDX) and Utility Dog (U-UD).

Obedience trials (the events where the competition is held), like conformation shows, are a wonderful place to socialize with friends, meet new people, share training methods, stories and enjoy the sport of dogs. Friendships have been formed at obedience and conformation events that have lasted lifetimes.

Although the goal of most obedience competitors is to earn obedience titles, the nice thing about this sport is you can make it what you want. If you are very competitive, you can compete with the goal to earn the very highest scores possible, winning trophies, ribbons and awards. However, if you are not quite so competitive, you can keep it lower keyed. Some people compete only in fun matches (to be explained later) where no titles are awarded; they compete strictly for fun. For those who do wish to earn titles but are not competitive, there is no need to feel bad about it; when the titles are awarded, nowhere on the certificate does it say what your scores were, so compete at a level comfortable for you.

The practical aspects of obedience training are, of course, of utmost importance. The basic commands mentioned in Chapter 4 are just the beginning. Advanced obedience training can make your Aussie a viable, working member of your household. Your Aussie will be happy to work—-its capabilities are limited only by your time, patience and ability to communicate.

Competing in Obedience

Dogs and owners competing in obedience are competing in two ways: they are judged by their performance against a set of exercise guidelines established by each

Lawson's Cool Shamus UD, ATDds, the twenty-fourth ASCA UD recorded and the 1985 ASCA National Specialty Most Versatile.

However, additional awards are available for the competitors who perform best when scored against the other competitors that day. Clubs hosting trials usually offer ribbons for first, second, third and fourth place competitors in each class and many clubs also offer rosettes, trophies or medallions. Some clubs even offer ribbons to all dogs earning qualifying scores. Special awards are available for high-scoring dogs in each breed, for high-scoring conformation champion, and so on. There is also a special award for the dog that earns the highest score of the day, all the classes combined. This High in Trial award is equivalent to a conformation Best in Show award.

The Novice Class

If you decide to tackle obedience competition, you and your Aussie will begin competing at the Novice level. The Novice A class is for beginning dogs and beginning owners. Novice B is for dogs that have not earned an obedience title but whose owner/handler or professional trainer have earned obedience titles with other dogs.

Your Aussie can earn an AKC Companion Dog title (CD) by competing in the Novice class at AKC obedience trials. Or your dog can earn an ASCA CD at ASCA trials or a U-CD at United Kennel Club (UKC) trials. If you find you and your Aussie both enjoy training and competing, go for all three.

There are some variations between the AKC, UKC and ASCA competitions. The AKC trials are the most popular, with more trials held and more dogs attending; therefore, the

registry and they are competing against the other competitors. Every competitor that passes all the exercises in its class (earning more than half of all points in each exercise, totaling 170 or more points out of the 200 available) earns a qualifying score, or "leg" towards its obedience title. Three of these qualifying scores are required under three different judges to earn a title.

The long sit.

AKC rules will be explained first. (Any variations found in ASCA or UKC exercises will explained following the AKC exercise descriptions. To make sure you understand the exercises and rules for competition and for any changes that may have been recently instituted, write to the registries under which you will be competing for the guidelines concerning obedience competition.)

In AKC Novice, you and your Aussie will be required to pass six different exercises to earn a qualifying score. The first exercise is the Heel on Leash, where your dog must walk with you, adapting its pace to yours, walking at a normal speed, slow and fast, as well as making left, right and about turns and a figure eight. Your Aussie does not pass this exercise if it is unmanageable, tugs or pulls on the leash, urinates or defecates in the ring or if you are constantly changing pace to walk with the dog.

In the second exercise, your Aussie will have to do a Stand for Exam, off-leash. In this exercise your dog is told to stand and

stay. After you tell your dog to stay, you must walk six feet away, turn and face your dog while the judge walks up to it and touches it on the head, shoulders and hips. The dog must remain in position until you walk back to the heel position next to your dog and the judge says, "Exercise finished." Your dog does not pass if it moves from position, sits or lays down, or shows shyness or resentment. Any dog that growls or threatens the judge or bites will be excused from the ring. If a dog is excused twice, it is barred from any further competition.

The heel position. Heeling is a fundamental exercise at all levels of obedience competition.

The third exercise is the Heel Free, or heel off-leash. The exercise is the same as the heel on leash, except your Aussie is off the leash. Scoring is much the same as the Heel on Leash.

The fourth exercise is the Recall. In this exercise, your Aussie must demonstrate it will wait in one place when you walk away and will come directly to you, sitting in front of you, when you call it to come. The emphasis in this exercise is a solid wait and a fast come. The dog will fail the exercise if it refuses to come or needs more than one command to come, or if it moves from position before you call.

The fifth and sixth exercises are both stays. The sit/stay is for one minute and the down/stay is for three minutes. In both exercises, your Aussie will be lined up along one side of the ring with other dogs and when instructed by the judge, you and the other owners will leave your dogs, walking across the ring, turning to face the dogs while the judge times the exercise. The emphasis in this exercise is a solid stay.

The ASCA Novice class is the same as the AKC class; however, the UKC Novice has a few differences. In UKC Novice, the down/stay is called an honoring exercise. The dog doing the down/stay must do so while the next dog is performing its heelwork. The sit/stay is the same as in AKC Novice. Another difference is in the recall exercise. In the UKC Novice, the dog will be called to come and when it does so, it must jump over a hurdle that is between the dog and its owner.

The front.

The broad jump.

The Open Class

After your Aussie has earned its CD, it is eligible to go on to the Open A or B Class, where it can earn a Companion Dog Excellent (CDX) title. Open A is for dogs that have not yet earned the Companion Dog Excellent title and must be handled by the owner or a member of the owner's immediate family. Unlike Novice A, even if an owner has earned a degree with another dog, he or she may still compete in the Open A class with a beginning dog. Open B is for professional trainers, or owners who have earned a Companion Dog Excellent title or an Obedience Trial Championship on a dog. Any dog with at least a Companion Dog Title may compete in the Open B Class. There are seven exercises in Open and the guidelines for a qualifying score are the same as in Novice: your Aussie must earn over half of all points available in each exercise, totaling 170 or more. A qualifying score equals one "leg" and each dog must earn three legs under three different judges to earn a CDX.

The first exercise in AKC Open is the Heel Free and Figure Eight. This is similar to the Novice Heel Free except the figure eight is performed off-leash, whereas in Novice, the figure eight was on leash. The emphasis is on your dog's attention on you, its willingness to work and your off-leash control. Scoring is the same as in Novice.

The second exercise is the Drop on Recall. This is very much like the Recall in Novice, except your Aussie must drop (lay down in place) on command while it is moving towards you as you call it to come. The emphasis in this exercise is a fast come, a quick drop in place and another fast come from the drop. Scoring is the same as in Novice except that your dog can fail if it does not drop on the first command, or if it anticipates the drop, or if it does not come to you when you call it to come after the drop.

The third Open exercise is the Retrieve on the Flat. Your Aussie must wait by your side in the heel position while you throw a

Retrieve over the high jump.

Dickson's Bob, the first ASCA UD.

The fifth exercise is the Broad Jump. Your Aussie must wait in position in front of the jump as you walk away and position yourself to the side of the jump. On your signal or command, the dog must jump over the Broad Jump, turn and come back to you, sitting in front of you. The dog can fail if it walks across the jump, fails to jump, does not come back to you or anticipates your command to jump. The emphasis in this exercise is on the jump.

The sixth and seventh exercises in Open are the stays; a three minute sit/stay and a five minute down/stay, similar to Novice except when the owners leave their dogs on the judge's instructions, they will walk across the ring and then leave the ring, walking to a pre-set position out of the dogs' sight. They will not return to their dogs until called by the judge at the end of the time allowed. The emphasis in these two exercises is a solid stay, even when your dog cannot see you.

The ASCA Open Class is the same as the AKC and again, there are a few differences in the UKC exercises. The down/stay is an Honoring exercise while another dog is working in the ring. As with the AKC class, the owner will leave the ring so that the down/stay is done with the owner out of sight. Another change is in the Heel Off-leash exercise. While your Aussie is heeling, a ring steward (the judge's assistant) will walk a pre-set pattern across the ring, acting as a distraction. There is a walking steward in the Drop on Recall exercise, too. During the Drop on Recall, after your Aussie drops on command, a steward will walk toward the dog. After the steward passes the dog, the judge will then instruct you to call your dog to you.

dumbbell. On your command, the dog must leave your side, going directly to the dumbbell, pick it up and bring it back to you, holding it until you take it from your dog. The emphasis in this exercise is on the retrieve. Your Aussie can fail if it anticipates your command to retrieve, fails to retrieve or drops the dumbell before you take it.

The fourth exercise is the Retrieve over the High Jump. The exercise is the same as the retrieve on the flat except your Aussie must jump a high jump going out to the dumbbell and after picking up the dumbell, bring it back to you. The dog can fail the exercise if it fails to retrieve or if it does not jump either direction. The emphasis in this exercise is on both the retrieve and the jump.

The Utility Class

After completing a CDX title, you and your Aussie can compete in the Utility Class. The Utility Class is divided into A & B, the same as in the Open Class. Utility A has the same requirements as Open A, except that your Aussie must have earned the Companion Dog Excellent title (CDX). Any dog with at least a Companion Dog Excellent title may compete in the Utility B class. Three qualifying scores (or legs) in the Utility class will earn your Aussie the UD title from either the ASCA or AKC, or the U-UD from the UKC. Utility, often jokingly call "futility" by some competitors, can be difficult. The exercises are more complicated for the owner to teach and more difficult for your Aussie to learn. However, the sense of accomplishment you will feel after earning a UD is unsurpassed.

The AKC Utility class has five exercises. The first is the Signal exercise. No verbal commands are allowed in this exercise, all commands must be hand signals. Your Aussie must know, recognize and respond to signals to heel, stand, sit, stay, drop, come and finish. Your Aussie will fail the exercise if it does not respond to the signals or if it does not perform the exercises correctly.

The second exercise is Scent Discrimination. Your Aussie will have to search out and find, one at a time, a metal and a leather article that you have touched so they carry your scent. By sniffing the articles, your dog will be able to identify those articles carrying your scent from among identical articles that the ring steward has touched. Your dog will fail if it does not retrieve each of the articles, if it brings back the wrong article, or if it refuses to work.

Scent discrimination, searching for the correct article.

Scent discrimination, success.

The hand signal for the Utility directed jump exercise.

The third exercise is the Directed Retrieve. In this exercise, three cotton gloves (supplied by you) will be placed along one side of the ring. One glove will be placed in each corner and one in the middle;the judge will indicate which glove must be retrieved. You will send your dog to the correct glove by turning toward the glove, having your Aussie sit in the heel position after you turn, and then sending your dog to the correct glove. The dog will fail the exercise if it brings back the wrong glove or if it fails to retrieve at all.

The fourth exercise is the Moving Stand and Examination. While walking forward with your Aussie at a heel, you will tell it to stand and continue walking forward ten to twelve feet. Your Aussie must stop in place at your command. The judge will then walk up to the dog and exam it quite thoroughly. When he has finished, you will then call your dog to heel. The dog can fail the exercise if it does not hold the stand, if it sits or lays down from the stand or if it shows resentment toward the judge during the exam.

The last exercise in the AKC Utility Class is the Directed Jumping. Your Aussie must, at your signal or command, run straight across the ring and, again at your command, turn and sit. The judge will then direct you to send your dog over either the high jump or the bar jump. After the first jump, you will send your Aussie out again and send it over the other jump. The dog will fail if it refuses to jump either jump, refuses to run across the ring or touches or climbs the jumps when jumping over them.

As with Novice and Open, the ASCA Utility Class is the same as the AKC. In the UKC Utility Class an Honoring exercise, with the Honoring dog doing a down/stay while the other dog works is included. The UKC Signal and Scent Discrimination Exercises are very similar to the AKC exercises, except in Scent Discrimination there is one retrieve required, with metal articles only; whereas in the AKC exercise your Aussie must retrieve twice, once for a metal article and once for a leather.

The UKC Directed Retrieve Exercise is split into two different exercises, the Directed (Marked) Retrieve and the Directed (Signal) Retrieve. The gloves are positioned differently, too, with one glove halfway down the right side of the ring, one halfway down the left side and the other glove midway across the far side of the ring. In the Marked Retrieve exercise you will send your Aussie as you did in the AKC Directed Retrieve, turning toward the glove and sending the dog after it. In the Directed Signal Retrieve, you will send your Aussie away from you across the ring,

Brigadoon's Sweptaway CGC, CDX, a multiple High in Trial winning dog and the first Aussie to score a perfect 200 at an AKC Obedience Trial.

and then have it turn and sit, as you did in the AKC Directed Jumping Exercise. At the judge's command, you will then send your Aussie to one of the gloves.

The UKC Consecutive Recall is a combination of the AKC Novice Recall and the AKC Open Recall. Your Aussie must first do a Drop on Recall, as in Open, followed by a straight Recall, with no drop, as in Novice.

After your Aussie completes its Utility Dog title, it may now compete for two additional titles from AKC, Utility Dog Excellent (UDX) and Obedience Trial Champion (OTCH).

Utility Dog Excellent

This title is earned after your Aussie has received ten separate qualifying scores in both the Open B and Utility B classes. This title is not required to achieve the Obedience trial championship from AKC discussed below.

Obedience Trial Champion

The American Kennel Club (AKC) and the Australian Shepherd Club of America (ASCA) offer the title of Obedience Trial Champion (OTCH) to dogs that have completed their Utility Dog title (UD) and that continue to compete in Open B and Utility B classes and that have satisfied the requirements for Obedience Trial Champion.

To earn an AKC OTCH, your Aussie must earn a first place in Open B, a first place in Utility B and a first place in either Open B or Utility B, all under different judges. In addition to the class placements your dog must accumulate a total of 100 points; the points are awarded according to the number of dogs competing in the classes where your Aussie places either first or second.

To earn an ASCA OTCH, an Aussie must earn 100 points, awarded according to the number of dogs defeated. In addition, it must also earn a score of 193 or higher from Open B, one score of 193 or higher from Utility and one score of 195 or higher from either Open B or Utility B.

The Non-Regular Classes

There are a couple of other classes you and your Aussie can compete in but titles are not available for these classes; they are simply for fun and practice.

The Subnovice or Novice Y class is for dogs that are starting to compete but are not yet ready for Novice. All of the exercises, including the heel, stand, come and stays, are

VCH WTCH Ch. Gold Nugget's Cock of the Walk, CD, TD

Ch. Propwash Two Up CD.

on leash. There are no off-leash exercises. This class allows dogs to get used to the ring situation before being taken off-leash. Because this is a practice class, it is offered at matches but not at trials.

The Graduate Novice class is for dogs that have completed a CD but are not yet ready for Open. The Heel on Leash and Stand for Exam are the same as in Novice but the Heel Free, Drop on Recall and Sit and Down Stays are the same as in Open. This class is offered at most matches and is sometimes offered at trials hosted by dog training clubs.

The Brace class is a lot of fun. One handler competes working two dogs at the same time, side by side. The exercises are the same as in Novice, as is the scoring. The goal is that the dogs should demonstrate how well they can work in unison.

The Team class consists of four dogs and four handlers, competing in the ring at the same time. The goal of this class is to have all four handlers and dogs work in unison, much like a drill team.

The Veterans class is for dogs that are seven years or older. These seniors may have earned any obedience title, up to and including OTCh. The exercises performed are the same as in the Novice class, even if the dog has earned a title higher than CD. The Veterans class is a great way for the older dog to get some attention it might otherwise miss, sitting at home while the younger dogs compete. Many a tear is wiped away at ringside when the old dogs strut their stuff.

Preparing for Competition

You and your Aussie will need to do some training prior to entering your first obedience match or trial. Not only will it need to know the exercises described above, but you will also need to be familiar with the rules pertaining to competition. These rules are explained in the written guidelines available from each registry.

The "watch me" command.

The long down.

OTCH U-UD Moriah Farm Victoria

"RIA"

OWNER: CARY HUNKEL
BREEDER: WENDY AND RANDY DAGGETT

"Ria was my first dog and was bought to be a pet, a housedog. We were told that Aussies are smart enough to get into trouble if they are not directed, so we enrolled in an obedience training class. That one class hooked me on training!" Cary said.

Ria has been High Scoring Australian Shepherd seventeen times, High Scoring Dog in Trial five times and has won High Combined four times. She earned her OTCH in 1993 and qualified for the Front & Finish Super Utility Award.

"Ria is more than just a super obedience dog;" said Cary "she also competes in scent hurdle races where she shows her herding instinct by circling the box with the dumbbells five times before grabbing the right one. She loves to play Frisbee and go swimming. She likes to play in the snow and pulls a sled loaded with kids. We also go skijouring; it's a blast to have her pull me on cross-country skis."

"Ria is fun and entertaining, has been a great obedience partner and has, without a doubt, hooked me on dogs, Aussies in particular!"

You can prepare for competition by training alone or you can train with other people. Dog training clubs are a great place to train because you can talk to people involved in the same sport. Dog training clubs are also ideal places to share training methods and ideas and ask questions of people who have more experience than you. If you cannot find a training club near you, there are many dog training books available to help you work alone.

When you think you and your Aussie have mastered the Novice exercises, you can enter a fun or practice match. As was explained in the previous chapter, matches are similar to a show except they are for practice only and titles cannot be awarded. In a match, you and your Aussie can learn the ring routine, how the judging works and simply get experience in the sport prior to entering a trial.

You can find out where and when matches are held by asking pet professionals: groomers, trainers, veterinarians, or by asking at local dog clubs. Many times dog clubs will mail out a newsletter listing upcoming events. In some parts of the country there are subscription newsletters listing dog activities. Again, ask other people involved in the sport.

Once you have attended several matches and you and your dog are both comfortable with the ring, the ring routine, the judging procedures and the regulations pertaining to competition, then it is time to enter a trial.

A Trial

The AKC requires you to pre-enter an obedience trial, which means you must find out about it ahead of time and mail in your entry blank and fee prior to the pre-entry deadline. Many UKC and ASCA clubs also require pre-entry, although some allow you to enter the day of the show or trial, the premium list or flyer announcing the trial will specifically tell you which applies.

If you pre-enter, you will receive an acknowledgment of your entry just prior to the trial. This will tell you what time your class judging will start and what your armband number is. Bring this information with you to the trial.

On the day of the trial, dress in comfortable clothes that are neat, clean and attractive. This is not the place for jeans with holes in the knees or a T-shirt with an offensive saying on the front. Wear comfortable shoes that will not slip in wet grass or give you blisters by the end of the day.

When you arrive at the trial, buy a catalog. This will list all of the dogs competing and their armband numbers, as well as the ring number for each class. Also listed are the judges for each class. Find your ring and check in with the steward prior to the start of judging: "Good morning. I am armband number 25." The steward will then give you your armband which you will wear on your left arm, on the bicep. Find out from the steward which dog you will follow into the ring, and then pay attention. Dogs listed in the catalog may be absent, so go by the steward's directions. If you do not show up when its your turn to be judged, the judge can mark you absent and you will lose your chance to compete. The judge does not have to allow you a later chance, although some judges will make an exception.

Watching the dogs that precede you will also give you a chance to become familiar with your judge's ring routine. Where does he have you start? Where is the heel pattern? Where does the judge position you for the recall? Although you do not have to memorize the judge's routine, you still must follow his directions; you will be more comfortable when you know what to expect.

Before and after competition—in fact, the entire time you are out in public—watch your dog. Do not let it sniff other dogs or bark or charge at other dogs. Keep your dog close to you. If it has to relieve itself, take it away from the rings and pick up after it. Be considerate of your fellow competitors and the groundskeepers who must clean up after the trial.

When the class is completed and winners are announced, be a good sport. Congratulate the winners and thank the judge. If you or your Aussie has a bad day, do not charge out of the ring jerking at the collar or yelling at your dog. Not only is that bad sportsmanship but your Aussie will not understand. In fact, this kind of behavior will be counterproductive for further training.

Keep in mind, obedience competition is a sport to be enjoyed. It does not matter if you are aiming for the perfect scores and the High in Trials or are simply working for a title. There will always be another day, another trial and another chance to succeed. So smile, enjoy your Aussie's company and be a good sport.

Celebrin Moonlighting CGC, UD, STDd, HC, AG-1, DWA, High in Trial at the USASA National Specialty, 1994 and three-time qualifier for the Gaines Obedience Competition.

Chapter 7

Herding Heritage

Most Experts Agree that the herding instinct seen in dogs today is derived from the hunting instincts of wolves and other wild canines. The fastest wolves would run to the front of a herd of deer, elk, reindeer, caribou or musk ox circling them to stop any forward movement. Members of the herd might try to escape but the circling wolves either would prevent escape or would allow one animal (usually sick, injured, very young or very old) to drop behind so that it could be caught. Even today, occasionally a herding dog will become a stock killer. The reasons why a dog goes "bad" vary. One often-repeated theory is that the stock killer has regressed "back to its wolf heritage."

From the human perspective, this herding instinct is one of the most useful and valuable canine attributes. Through selective breeding, nomads created a partner that not only provided companionship and protection but also helped put food on the table by supervising and protecting the first domesticated herd animals. In return, the canine partner received food, a warm body to sleep with and shelter from the weather.

Herding Dogs Today

Although some Australian Shepherds are lucky enough to live on working farms, most are not. This change in circumstances has reduced many dogs, with a heritage of centuries of working instincts, to pacing back and forth across city sized yards, herding other pets or even children out of frustration. This frustration often leads to behavior problems such as barking, digging up the yard, nipping at children or jumping a fence. Fortunately, many opportunities for recreational herding are now available, allowing your Aussie a chance to use its instincts and run off excess energy. Also, or it can be used in herding trials, competing for trophies, titles, and some-times, even money. Herding trials, in fact, are one of the most popular and fastest growing canine sports. More than five thousand dogs of various breeds compete each year in the United States in formal trials. In addition, many communities have training facilities where novice dogs and novice handlers can experience the fun of herding livestock under the guidance of herding instructors.

Be sure your stock dog has an abundant water supply.

Simply stated, herding is using a dog to control or move livestock. This simple defini-tion does not begin to describe the variety of breeds of dogs with numerous working characteristics involved in herding. The pure breeds most often seen at ASCA and AKC herding trials are Australian Cattle Dogs, Bearded Collies, Belgian Sheepdogs, Belgian Tervuren, Border Collies, Shetland Sheepdogs, Corgis, and, of course, Australian Shepherds. And the events themselves vary in type and com-plexity. Opportunities are available for dog and handler to participate in simple activities such as a Herding Instinct Test, where little more is required than for an Aussie to demonstrate its herding instincts, or something as complex as the ASCA National, where dogs may compete against other expert herding Aussies for High in Trial awards on Ducks, Sheep and Cattle.

Aussies work all types of stock.

Herding Dog Characteristics

An Aussie's inborn herding abilities are a vital part of the character of the breed. These abilities, properly nurtured, can become virtues sought after by rancher and trial handler alike. Whether you are working an Aussie on a ranch, showing a competitive trial dog, or working your Aussie on weekends for fun, your dog must demonstrate the same abilities. Many Australian Shepherds work on a farm all week and compete successfully on the weekends.

In addition to an Aussie's instinctive capabilities, it must also be fit. It must be sound physically, able to work all day, often with only occasional rest breaks. A dog that has hip or elbow dysplasia,

vision problems or is not conformationally sound, will not be able to do the job. An Aussie must be able to accelerate, turn on a dime, and jump with considerable agility. A hard-working dog also needs to learn how to pace itself, using its strength and energy efficiently. If a dog goes like wild horses for the first hour, and then is tired by its third hour working, it will be useless by the end of the day.

Before starting your Aussie herding stock, you need to know what characteristics are useful in a herding dog and the terms associated with this sport and profession. Certain characteristics are fundamental to the nature of an effective herding dog. Aussies'

personalities and temperaments may differ, but to some degree they must all possess two traits: trainability and instinctive Force or Power. Your Aussie's ability to work stock effectively is enhanced by these traits and by other factors. A balanced combination of traits will complement the training your Aussie receives and make it successful at whatever type of work it is used for.

An illegal grip. Gripping, when necessary, is allowed only on the nose and at the rear "heels" of stock.

TRAINABILITY

Often called "biddability," trainability is your dog's ability to be taught and take commands. Your Aussie's trainability can make or break it. All the instincts in the world are no good to you if your Aussie does not want to work for you, will not take your direction and commands, and refuses to accept your authority.

FORCE OR POWER

Good herding dogs possess a presence or power that allows them to control the stock. This power, or force, is shown in different ways. Some dogs bark as a means of showing power. Barking can be good when a dog is trying to move a large herd, especially cattle, or when a dog is trying to turn a herd of runaways. However, barking can also be a sign of weakness in a dog. Many insecure or young dogs yap or bark too much. Barking can be counterproductive when a dog is working nervous stock animals that might panic. A good working dog barks only when necessary.

An Aussie's bearing or demeanor conveys power. Your Aussie can make its presence known by its approach to the stock, and by the distance at which it works the stock, either close in or farther out. By

Showing strong "Eye."

varying the distance and direction of its approach your Aussie can show its power.

The "grip" is also known as a show of force or power. Some Aussies nip or bite the heels of the stock, especially cattle, to get the herd or an individual animal moving. Although a certain amount of gripping is fine, an Aussie that bites indiscriminately or without self-restraint can damage or kill stock. Gripping can also be the sign of an inexperienced dog that does not know how to move stock without gripping. As with restraint in barking, a good working Aussie will grip only when necessary.

Another way of showing force or power, used by many good herding dogs is eye. Border Collies are noted for their use of eye. Border Collies stalk livestock with head lowered in a predatory stance, staring intently at the stock. Although Aussies do not always exhibit eye the way a Border Collie does, it is a beneficial trait: it helps a dog concentrate and conveys power. However, more eye is not necessarily better; the use of eye must be balanced with the overall ability of an Aussie to move stock.

" 'Way to me" command—the counterclockwise movement of the dog around the stock.

Basic Herding Commands and Terms

COMMANDS

Commands vary depending upon the trainer/handler, the stockman, the part of the country you are from and/or the type of work you and your Aussie will do. Listed below are a few common commands, as well as commonly used stockdog terms and their definitions.

Away to Me or 'Way to Me: Move in a counter-clockwise direction around the stock (The direction is based on the dog facing toward the handler and stock).

Mistretta's Firefly (at 10 weeks) shows his working instinct.

Come By or Go By: Move in a clockwise direction around the sheep (The direction is based on the dog facing to the handler and stock).

Come: Come directly to the handler (The command can also be used as a shortened Come By command, directing an Aussie to move clockwise around the stock).

Easy or Steady: Slow down.

Lie Down or Down: Lie down or drop in place.

Look Back: To look behind for stock it has missed or that have moved out of its sight.

Get Back or Get Out or Get Back Out: Move out and away from the stock, or work farther out from the stock. Get back can also mean for a dog to back up away from its existing position.

"Walk up" command—the dog walks slowly towards the stock.

Stand or Stand There: Stop, stand still and hold its position on the stock.

That'll Do: Stop what it is doing. That'll do often comes before another command, such as That'll do, come or That'll do, lie down.

There: Stop and hold its position. It may lie down or stand until given another command.

Walk Up or Walk On: Walk towards the stock.

HERDING TERMINOLOGY

Balance: The position your Aussie will choose to hold stock together most effectively, usually at the 6 O'clock and 12 O'clock position in relation to the handler.

Cross Drive: Moving stock across an area, from one obstacle to another.

Drive: Moving the stock away from you.

Fetch: After the lift your dog will move the stock toward you. The dog will keep the stock between itself and you.

A missing front leg does not diminish this Aussie's ability to work.

"Come-by" command—the clockwise movement of the dog around the stock. This dog also shows strong eye.

Flanking: Circling or moving around the sheep either in a clockwise or in a counter-clockwise direction.

Gather: Bringing stock together from scattered positions, into a group.

Headers and Heelers: There are basically two categories of herding dogs: headers and heelers. Headers run ahead of the stock to stop the forward motion or head them. These dogs also known as fetching or gathering dogs, will often naturally turn the stock and bring them to the owner. The heeler (or driving dog) will keep the stock moving as a group. These dogs normally work at the back of the herd, using their "power" to move the herd forward, and also moving from right to left (wearing) to keep the stock together. Aussies work as both headers and heelers. Obviously a dog that can use both methods proficiently is more versatile and more valuable for both work and sport.

Lift: The moment when your Aussie has completed its outrun, and makes contact with the stock before starting the fetch.

Outrun: Your Aussie running out toward the stock in a wide arch or pear-shaped semi-circle, positioning itself behind the stock, opposite you in the balance position.

Pen or Penning: Moving stock into an enclosure.

Post or Handler's Post: A post in the ground indicating the position where the handler must stand while giving commands.

Aussies are used on the farm for many herding tasks, such as moving stock out of barns and...

Pressure Point: The point at which your Aussie can most efficiently get a herd to move, by applying pressure or showing its power.

Shed: Separating one or a group of livestock from a herd and holding them apart from the main herd.

Wearing: The side-to-side movement of a dog to hold stock together.

The Working Farm Dog

As a working farm dog, an Australian Shepherd has to be versatile enough to do a number of different chores, including penning or holding stock, moving or driving the stock from one location to another and gathering stock together. An Aussie should be gentle enough to handle lambs, hard enough to handle range cattle, and smart enough to work cows with calves. Depending on the season, a dog will need to work in rain, fog, snow and sleet, the cold of winter and the heat of summer. A working dog will be bothered by fleas, ticks, flies and mosquitoes, by foxtails, burrs, gravel and dust.

The primary purpose of a working farm dog is to save time, effort and man-hours. To do this, an Aussie should be able to do several different tasks which may include gathering or rounding up stock such as dairy cows to be

...moving stock from one pasture to another and...

116

...driving stock from one location to another.

milked; holding sheep in an area for shearing; driving a herd from a pasture to a barn and back; shedding, or separating an individual from the main herd for veterinary care; and penning or moving stock into an enclosed area such as a corral or holding pen.

An Aussie should have the ability to make an outrun of great distance, lift the stock without scattering them, and fetch or gather the stock directly back to the farmer. A farm Aussie will know when to apply pressure, using its natural power and presence to effectively and efficiently complete its job.

The Australian Shepherd Club of America offers a Ranch Dog Certification (RD) program to promote and recognize working farm Aussies. This certificate can be earned by an Aussie that assists its owner in daily

farm life. The test is given on an individual basis and an Aussie will either pass or fail; no point scores are given. The test is based on what a dog does in its normal duties, which will be different for each dog.

The Ranch Trial Program is another certification to recognize working farm Aussies. The Ranch Trial program is open to Aussies who have earned an Open Trial Dog Certificate or an Advanced Trial Dog Certificate (see below) in either the sheep or cattle class, or to an Aussie that has received its Ranch Dog (RD) certification. To earn the Ranch Trial Dog Certificate (RTD) your Aussie need only receive one qualifying score at a ranch dog

WTCH Ramblin Rose Texas Gambler RDX competing at the ASCA National Specialty Stockdog Finals, 1993.

117

Above, Penning stock during an ASCA competition.

Below, Moving the stock out after penning.

The top ten finalists at the ASCA National Specialty 1990.

trial (75 points of a possible 100), in the stock class entered (only sheep and cattle classes are available at Ranch Trials). Ranch Trials are held on working farms and ranches, and because of this, no two ranch trials are exactly the same. Ranch Trials include moving stock from one pen to another, sorting or separating stock, moving stock through a loading chute and gathering and driving stock through a pasture.

The Competitive Herding Dog

ASCA Stockdog Program

In the United States, ASCA has offered stockdog trials and titles for a number of years. The ASCA guidelines state that the objectives of the Stockdog Program are: "To preserve the natural inherited working abilities of the Australian Shepherd. To stimulate interest in and recognize the working ability of the breed by use of the Certification Program and to keep a

permanent record on file of the working dog's accomplishments that will prove helpful in improved breeding practices."

ASCA offers several stockdog titles or certifications, in three divisions or levels of competition. Each level is divided into classes based on the type of livestock to be worked: ducks (d), sheep (s) or cattle (c).

The Started Division is the first level, which is for Aussies six months or older, who have not yet earned certification in the stock class being entered. After receiving two qualifying scores from two different judges (69 points of a possible 100) in the stock class entered, the Aussie earns the Started Trial Dog certification or STD.

Moving stock through the center panels on an ASCA stockdog course.

The second division is Open and is for Aussies who have earned certification in the Started Division for the stock class entered. An Aussie again must receive two qualifying scores from two different judges (88 points of a possible 125 and at least 40 percent of the total coarse score) for the class of stock entered to earn its Open Trial Dog Certification or OTD.

The final level is Advanced and this division is for Aussies who have earned certification in the Open Division. The Aussie must receive two qualifying scores from two different judges (88 points of a possible 125 and at least 50 percent of the total coarse score), which will give it an Advance Trial Dog certification, or ATD. Aussies who have earned the ATD may continue to compete in the Advanced classes.

An Aussie does not need to earn certification on all classes of livestock. However, all class certifications must be earned in order: Started, Open and Advanced. For example, if

Moving stock through panels on an ASCA stockdog course.

an Aussie earns its Started Certification in the duck class (STDd), it must then earn its Open Certification (OTDd) before moving to the Advanced division, duck class to earn its Advanced Certification, ducks (ATDd). This same process must be followed for sheep and cattle classes.

Classes in each of the above divisions can be run on one of two courses, A or B. The course layouts in a division are the same for each class of livestock; the difficulty of the elements and the work your Aussie must perform is increased with each division.

On course A, your Aussie should be able to take stock from a pen and move or drive the stock counterclockwise around the arena, through a set of panels (or fencing), across the arena between another set of panels, and finally drive the stock down the center of the arena, through a "chute" (panels set parallel to each other). When the exercises are complete, an Aussie must be able to "re-pen" (put the

An Aussie should be able to re-pen the stock at the end of a course run.

120

WTCH The Bull of Twin Oaks CD, RDX, RTDs

"The Bull"

OWNER: CEE HAMBO

BREEDER: AUDREY KLARER

Cee says about The Bull, "I work The Bull on my ranch but the work isn't very pretty, just efficient. I run about thirty registered Brahman, plus my family has about 300 Brahman crosses. The Brahman is quite a bit smarter and quicker than the average cow. When The Bull is working for me, with these cattle, he must be able to think for himself and he does, sometimes too much so!"

Sherry Baker trained and trialed The Bull. She is second generation Twin Oaks and has put WTCH titles on seven Twin Oaks dogs. Sherry agreed to trial The Bull because of her respect for his intelligence. He has won innumerable stock dog titles and awards, including: 1989 ASCA Champion Cattle Dog from the Stockdog Finals, 1990-1993 Top 10 Stock Dogs, plus numerous placements in the ASCA National Specialty Stock Dog Trials. His career was amazing and is making Australian Shepherd history.

The Bull is more than 'just' an award winning, working stock dog; he is also a gentle, well-loved therapy dog. Cee says, "If you could see him working a tough Brahman bull—see the aggression, the courage and the force that he has—and then see him with those old people in the nursing home, you wouldn't believe its the same dog. He truly is one of those amazing Aussies."

stock back in the pen it took them from). In the Open and Advanced Division, the handler must stand at a greater distance from the dog when giving commands and/or directions.

Course B requires that an Aussie perform a gather, then drive the stock clockwise through two panels, across the arena and between another set of panels. After the drive is completed, the dog must pen the stock in a fenced enclosure in the middle of the arena, take the stock out of the pen and finally "re-pen" the stock in the holding area. In the Open and Advanced division, the handler must remain behind the "handler's line," which is an imaginary boundary several yards away from the area the dog is be working.

In addition to the basic Stockdog titles of STD, OTD and ATD, ASCA offers the Working Trial Championship WTCH, which is awarded to dogs that have earned the Advanced Trial Dog certification in all three livestock classes (ducks, sheep and cattle). A Versatility Champion title and Supreme Versatility Champion title are awarded to dogs that have proven themselves in conformation competition, obedience competition and in stockdog work. To earn the Versatility Championship (VCH) title, an Aussie must earn its conformation championship, an obedience Companion Dog Excellent (CDX) title, and in herding, two Open Trial Dog Certifications (OTD) and one Advance Trial Dog Certification (ATD). The Supreme Versatility Championship (SVCH) title requires that an Aussie earn its

Ch. Bayshore's Three to Get Ready CD TT STDd showing his working ability.

conformation championship, its obedience Utility Dog title (UD) and a Working Trial Championship (WTCH).

For more information about ASCA's stockdog program and for a copy of the competition guidelines, write to ASCA at the address listed in Appendix A.

AKC Herding Program

In 1991, the AKC began a herding program with this stated purpose: "To preserve and develop the herding skills inherent in the herding breeds and to demonstrate that they can perform the useful function for which they were originally bred." The AKC program offers a variety of trial courses and levels of competition as well as Herding Tests that are non-competitive.

At each level of the AKC program your Aussie can earn a title, beginning with the non-competitive titles of Herding Tested (HT) and Pre-Trial Tested (PT). The next level of the program is the competitive trial classes at which the Herding Started (HS), Herding Intermediate (HI), Herding Advanced (HX) and Herding Championship (H. Ch.) titles are earned. Ducks, sheep and cattle are used in the tests and trial classes.

The Herding Tested (HT) Title. The HT was created to allow handlers to demonstrate an Aussie's natural herding instinct: the control of stock and moving stock in a pre-set pattern. This test is non-competitive and dogs are scored on a pass or fail basis. An Aussie must stop or pause on command, make two changes of direction controlling the movement of the stock and finally stop at the completion of the course and recall back to the handler. To receive an HT your Aussie must pass the test twice, judged by two different judges.

Pre-Trial Tested (PT) Title. This test is designed to help novice handlers understand herding tests and trials, and to develop the skills necessary to compete at trial level. The test demonstrates an Aussie's capability of performing herding work just below the beginning trial level. The PT is also noncompetitive and is scored on a pass or fail basis. In this test a handler must demonstrate that his or her Aussie is able to perform herding work just below the trial level. The test consists of a pause in the process of moving the stock through gates by

making a change in direction, and a stop when moving the stock toward a pen. At the conclusion of the exercises a dog must recall back to the handler. To received a PT an Aussie must pass the test twice, judged by two different judges.

The competitive herding titles are divided into three classes: Started (HS), Intermediate (HI) and Advanced (HX). To earn a title your Aussie must earn three

WTCH Windsong's Shenanigan CD, ASCA Hall of Fame Dam.

qualifying scores (a qualifying score being 60 points or more of a possible 100, with not less that 50 percent of the points possible in a single category) at three different trials, being judged by three different judges. The titles need not be earned in order; however, once your Aussie earns a qualifying score in an upper class, it may no longer compete in a lower class.

For each of the three classes stated above, there are three courses that can be used. The courses are A, B and C, elements are added to the courses and the difficulty of existing elements are increased for each level of competition.

On Course A an Aussie must be able to perform basic herding exercises such as an outrun, lift and fetch. It should be able to move or drive stock through panels set in different configurations, and in the upper classes it should be able to hold stock in an enclosure. Also, intermediate and advanced classes require that you give commands to your dog from a greater distance. Ducks, sheep or cattle can be used for course A classes.

Course B classes use sheep or ducks. An Aussie will again need to know basic exercises such as an outrun, lift and fetch, which are performed in succession. The dog must demonstrate the ability to take commands at a distance, to move or drive the stock between fence panels and across the arena as well as to hold the stock in a enclosure. In the advanced class, B course, an Aussie should know how to shed, or separate an individual from the herd and to hold them apart for a short period of time.

Only sheep are used on Course C classes which require an Aussie to work in a slow, steady fashion, moving the sheep at an unhurried casual pace from one grazing location to another. The sheep must be driven over a bridge, across a road, and then held in an open area.

After your Aussie has completed the HX title, it is now eligible to compete for a Herding Champion Certificate (H. Ch.). AKC offers this to dogs who have earned the HX title, and have earned a total of fifteen points in advanced classes at herding trials, with at least two first place finishes. Points are earned by placing first, second, third or fourth in the advanced classes, and the number of points awarded for each placement is based upon the number of dogs in competition. The maximum number of points awarded per show is five. An Aussie may continue to compete in advanced classes after it has earned a Herding Championship.

For complete details about the AKC herding program write to the AKC to request a current copy of the General Regulations for Herding Tests and Herding Trials; see Appendix B for the address. There are also herding tests and trials held all over the country, sponsored by different groups, some with substantial cash prizes. For more information about some of these programs, write to the Ranch Dog Trainer, Route 2, Box 333, West Plains, MO 65775.

Chapter 8

Versatility Is the Name of the Game

⊰⇒◦⇐⊱

WITH THEIR "let's do it!" attitude, trainability and natural athletic abilities, Australian Shepherds have excelled in many dog sports. If you and your Aussie enjoy training and cherish your time spent together, then check out some of these different activities and see what strikes your fancy. With most of these sports, you can use the activity as a training challenge, fun or as a competitive sport. A few of the activities, like search and rescue, or therapy dogs, are not sports at all but are serious, worthwhile, rewarding careers.

Agility

Agility is an active sport that is a combination of a child's playground, a grand prix jumping course—like that for horses—and a law enforcement dog obstacle course. Your Aussie must run through tunnels, leap over jumps of different heights and shapes and climb obstacles.

Agility training helps develop your dog's body awareness; the dog learns where its feet are and how to know where to step, jump or climb, and the dog becomes more aware of its

balance. An Aussie involved in agility training also gains confidence, both in itself and its abilities, and in you.

Agility training is also good for you, as your dog's trainer. You learn how to communicate with your Aussie, showing it what you want it to do. After all, your dog has no idea why you want it to jump through a strange-looking tire jump when it is so much easier to go around.

Although any dog can train in agility, an athletic, agile, confidant Australian Shepherd is perfect for the sport. Agility competition does require a physically fit dog and owner. To compete, your Aussie will first need obedience training to insure that you have reliable off-leash control.

Above, The bar jump.
Below, A variety of jump types are used on Agility courses.
Below, Right, The tire jump.

A dog enjoying his day. (Steve Eltinge)

Breeding your Aussie requires careful thought. In addition to physical appearance, other factors, such as health, genetic background and temperament of each parent, should be considered. (Steve Eltinge)

Cloverhill Propwash Bustle, whose coloring is called black-tri. (Steve Eltinge)

Everyone's having fun! (Steve Eltinge)

Ch. Brigadoon's California Dude CD, HI at ten years of age. He was Winners Dog and Best of Winners at the ASCA National Specialty, 1985. (Leida Jones)

An example of red merle coloring on an Aussie. (Steve Eltinge)

Aussies love to perform. (Steve Eltinge)

Moonlights Ruler of the Roost, a red merle. (Steve Eltinge)

This white-faced bitch exhibits no genetic problems; however, there is a high probability that puppies from a merle to merle breeding who exhibit "pattern white" markings will develop deafness and/or eye disorders. (Steve Eltinge)

Ch. Starswept's Out of the Blue, a blue merle. (Steve Eltinge)

Ch. Moonlights Roll Over Beethoven, a black-tri. (Steve Eltinge)

A couple of puppies. (J. Llapitan, Courtesy of Marge Stovall, Silverwood Australian Shepherds)

Grooming for a dog show requires time and skill. (Steve Eltinge)

Ch. Moonlights Hottest Thing Goin', Best of Breed at the ASCA National Specialty, 1993. (Steve Eltinge)

Watching his flock. (Steve Eltinge)

Mistretta's Rough Eagle STDdsc.
(Steve Eltinge)

FVF Ron D VU Riki of Carolot, a
red-tri-colored Aussie.
(Steve Eltinge)

Showdown! (Steve Eltinge)

A smile for the camera. (Steve Eltinge)

The one drawback to agility is that it does require equipment; but, if you have the room and the skills, you can build your own. If this is unrealistic, many dog training clubs or training schools now have agility equipment.

If you and Aussie enjoy agility training, you can earn agility titles in competition. The American Kennel Club offers a Novice Agility Dog (NAD) title, an Open Agility Dog (OAD) title, an Agility Dog Excellent (ADX) and a Master Agility Excellent (MAX). The United States Dog Agility Association offers the titles of Agility Dog, Advanced Agility Dog and Master Agility Dog.

Below, The A-frame.
Above Right, The dog walk.
Below Right, Training on the dog walk.

For information about the location of agility training clubs and agility competition, write to the AKC at the address listed in Appendix A, or to the U.S. Dog Agility Association, P.O. Box 850955, Richardson, TX 75085-0955. The North American Dog Agility Council (NADAC) also offers competition and titles, and may be reached at HCR 2 Box 277, St Maries, ID 83861. The Trans-National Club for Dog Agility is located at 401 Bluemont Circle, Manhattan, KS 66502-4531.

Canine Good Citizen

The AKC began the Canine Good Citizen program in hopes of combating some of the negative publicity surrounding dogs and dog owners. The AKC wanted to show the general public and the media that there are a lot of good dogs and responsible owners in local communities that are not normally in the media spotlight simply because they are not in trouble. Bad news is news! However, the AKC wants to promote good dogs and good owners and is doing so by establishing and promoting this program and by helping community clubs and dog trainers publicize the Canine Good Citizen tests.

Left, Accepting a friendly stranger.
Above, Sitting politely for petting.
Below, Appearance and grooming.

The Canine Good Citizen program (CGC) is open to all dogs, registered and nonregistered, pure-bred or mixed breed. The dog and owner take a short test, which does require some previous training. In the test, the dog must allow a stranger to approach the dog and the owner. The stranger will shake hands with you and greet your Aussie, which should not move from the sit by your side, should not jump on the stranger, growl, bark or misbehave in any other way. The dog must also allow someone to touch it, pet and groom it, and must remain in the sitting position by your side without exhibiting any shyness or resentment.

Above, Walk through a crowd.
Below Left, Walking on a leash.

You must also demonstrate that your Aussie will walk on a leash without pulling, even in a crowd situation, do a sit on command, a down and stay. You will then be allowed to praise your Aussie, play with it and get it excited, and then demonstrate that you can get it back under control, ready for the next part of the test. Next, your dog will be subject to several distractions, including another dog, a loud sound, such as a book being dropped, and a jogger dashing past. The last part of the test is supervised isolation. You will be asked to tie your dog and leave it under the judge's supervision while you go out of sight for five minutes. Your dog should not bark, whine, pace or howl.

Above, Sit on command.
Below, Down on command.
Right, Play interaction.

At the successful completion of the test, the dog is awarded a certificate that states it is a Canine Good Citizen and is entitled to use the initials "CGC" behind its name. The test is given by dog training clubs and dog trainers and is sometimes given at dog matches. If a local dog trainer does not offer the tests, write to the AKC for information about someone in your area who does.

The Temperament Test

Left, Reaction to another dog.
Above, Reaction to distractions.
Below, Supervised isolation.

Many Australian Shepherd owners and breeders emphasize they want more than just a pretty dog; they also want a dog that is intelligent and trainable. "A sound mind in a sound body." That phrase is the motto of the American Temperament Test Society (ATTS), a not-for-profit organization dedicated to the promotion of uniform temperament evaluation of all dogs. The ATTS trains testers and the other personnel required for a test and provides the format and guidelines for each test so tests are the same all over the country.

The ATTS test tries to duplicate, as much as possible, real-life situations and, as a result, gives breeders a way to measure the temperament of dogs that might be used in a breeding program. The test also gives pet owners a different look at their dog—how it might react in certain situations.

During the test, each dog is exposed to strangers—reserved, outgoing, weird and threatening—and the dog's responses are critiqued. The way a dog responds to various other visual and auditory stimuli such as loud and unusual sounds (including gunfire), and strange footing is also evaluated. When the dog is critiqued at the end of the test, certain factors are taken into consideration, including the breed of the dog and its hereditary purpose, the dog's training, age, gender and whether it is a house dog or kennel dog. During the critique, the owner is encouraged to ask questions regarding the dog's performance and reactions.

Dogs that pass the test are issued certificates and the title "TT." For more information about the American Temperament Test Society, write to ATTS, PO Box 397, Fenton, MO 63026.

Carting

Carting and draft dogs have been used by dog owners for thousands of years. Dogs have pulled sleds, wagons and travois, carrying or pulling home the results of a hunt, household furnishings, people or supplies. In many parts of the world, or in different cultures, horses, oxen or other large beasts of burden were not available or practical, but dogs were.

Today carting can be a fun sport with competitions much like driving horses. Breeds like Newfoundlands and Bernese Mountain Dogs are generally associated with carting competition but other breeds with the size, strength and endurance of an Aussie do very well. Competition aside, carting can be taught as a practical skill. When you go shopping and bring home a forty-pound bag of dog food, hook your dog up to its wagon and let it roll in the food. When the trash cans have to go out to the end of the driveway, load them in your Aussie's wagon.

For more information about carting, write to Dog Fancy Magazine, P.O. Box 6050, Mission Viejo, CA 92690 for back issue August 1988. On page sixty-five, the article "Putting the Dog Before the Cart" will help you train your Aussie. Dog World Magazine, 29 N. Wacker, Chicago, IL 60606 has an article called "Carting From A to Z" in its May 1992 issue, which is also very helpful.

Flyball is a fast-paced team relay sport and is especially fun for dogs that enjoy playing ball.

Flyball

Flyball is a team relay sport. Each team consists of four dogs and four owners. The dogs, one at a time, in a relay format, run and jump over a series of hurdles and then step on the lever of a box that throws a tennis ball. When your Aussie catches the ball, it then turns around and runs and jumps over the hurdles again, bringing the ball back to you, at which time the next dog starts. The team that finishes first, wins.

Flyball is especially fun for dogs that are tennis ball crazy; however, it does require some equipment. You will need four hurdles per team, plus one flyball box per team and you need at least four dogs and handlers for your team, as well as for other competing teams.

The North American Flyball Association offers titles for flyball competition. Flyball Dog (FD), Flyball Excellent (FDX) and Flyball Champion (FDCH) are available, all earned on a point system.

For more information, write to: North American Flyball Association, 1 Gooch Park Dr., Barrie, Ontario, Canada L4M 4S6. Write to Dog Fancy Magazine, PO Box 6050, Mission Viejo, CA 92690, ask for back issue August, 1990.

Frisbee

Frisbees are almost as popular with dogs as they are with people. Chasing a flying disc that swerves, climbs, banks and otherwise tantalizes the dog is even more fun than a tennis ball. (Frisbee is a trademarked name for a flying disc manufactured by Wham-O toys. For many, the word Frisbee has become synonymous with flying disc toys.)

If your Aussie is enthused about chasing a Frisbee, it can play for fun and exercise to use up some of that excess energy or it can chase a Frisbee in competition. Each year communities throughout the country sponsor local competitions for Frisbee catching canines. The dogs chase the flying discs, leap incredible heights to catch it and then chase it again. In addition, some Frisbee competitions include an

The versatile Aussie excels at many sports.

element of "freestyle" where a dog and handler perform amazing tricks to music—tricks that can include as many as five Frisbees. Regional competitions follow the community competitions and the winners go on to the World Finals.

Australian Shepherds have done very well in Frisbee competitions. Eldon McIntire and his late Australian Shepherd, Hyper Hank, were pioneers in the sport. McIntire and Hyper Hank performed their Frisbee magic at National Football League football game halftimes, including an exhibition at the Super Bowl XII. Bouncing Boo, owned by Bill Murphy, has won or placed at numerous World Finals, as have other Aussies. If you would like more information about Frisbee competition, call: Friskies Canine Frisbee Championships 818-780-4915 or 1-800-423-3268.

If your Aussie is motivated to jump, catch and retrieve but you have no interest in competition, you might consider using the soft, cloth discs now sold in most pet stores. These highly durable discs can be thrown with the same distance as hard plastic discs but are much safer for your dog and easier for them to pick up. Regrettably, the soft discs are not allowed in Frisbee competition.

To learn how to teach your Aussie to play Frisbee, ask for the following book at your library or book store: How to Teach Your Dog to Play Frisbee, by Karen Pryor, 1985, Simon and Schuster, New York. Write to Dog World Magazine, 29 N. Wacker, Chicago, IL 60606, asking for back issue January 1986. On page 10, the article "Frisbee—From A to Z" will help you teach Aussie to play the game.

Hiking and Packing

Do you like to go for walks in the country? Do you love the smell of a meadow in bloom in the spring? Or the smell of a pine forest after a rain? Is a weekend walk a good stress-reliever for you after a hard week at work? If so, then take your Aussie with you when you walk. The American Dog Packing Association is made up of dogs and owners who like to go hiking with their dogs. Some take day hikes, others go camping, backpacking and hiking.

Hiking is not competitive, however it is healthy, low impact exercise for both you and your dog. Short hikes, gradually increasing in length or difficulty, can help you and your Aussie get back into shape if you have both been couch potatoes. If your dog has been sedentary, be cautious, allowing it to slowly harden the pads of its feet and build its muscle tone. As your Aussie gets more fit, it can start wearing a dog pack, carrying water, first aid supplies and treats.

For more information, write to: The American Dog Packing Association, 2154 Woodlyn Rd., Pasadena, CA 91104.

Scent Hurdles

Scent hurdle racing is much like flyball, except that after your Aussie races over the hurdles, it must then use its nose and find the dumbbell that has your scent on it. Once your dog finds the correct dumbbell, it has to pick up the dumbell and return over the hurdles to you. Again, like flyball, scent hurdle racing is a team sport, with four dogs and handlers.

Aussies are great trail companions.

The first team to finish, wins. Contact your local dog trainer or dog training club to see if they have a team, or if they would be interested in starting a team.

Doggone Celebrin Indiana Jones CDX, HC, BH, TT learning the Schutzhund "guard and bark."

Schutzhund

The sport of schutzhund is German and was originally used to test military and law enforcement dogs, as well as working dogs, for suitability for breeding. In the United States, schutzhund is a competitive sport combining obedience, tracking and protection. As your Aussie competes in various levels, it can earn titles, including Schutzhund I, II and III. In addition, there are tests for endurance, traffic safety, drafting, companion dogs and watch dogs. Again,

your Aussie can earn titles in each area of competition. For example, the black tri Australian Shepherd, Kongo, has earned Schutzhund III (an advanced title), VB (Traffic Sure Dog), FH (Advanced Tracking), AD (drafting) and WH (watch dog.)

Some schutzhund clubs allow only the traditional German working dogs: German Shepherds, Rottweilers and Doberman Pinschers. Other clubs allow any dog capable of doing the work, and many Australian Shepherds have proven themselves very capable.

The first two Australian Shepherds to earn Schutzhund titles from the North American Working Dog Association (NASA) were ASCA Ch. Jones' Reddy Teddy Sch HA, CDX, STD, OTD, owned by Cathy Jones and Powder River's City Slicker AD owned by Jim Foster. Both of these dogs earned their schutzhund titles at a NASA-sanctioned trial in Fort Collins, Colorado on August 14, 1977.

Any dog that participates in schutzhund training must be of sound, stable temperament and physically fit. You, as the trainer, must take this training seriously. A protection or attack-trained dog is not a plaything but is a potentially dangerous weapon.

Ask at your library or book store for Beginners Guide to Schutzhund by Tom Mitchell, 1987, privately published, or Training the Competitive Working Dog by Tom Rose and Gary Patterson, 1985, Giblaut Publishing, Company. For more information, write: Landersverband DVG America, 113 Vickie Drive, Del City, OK 73115. Or: United Schutzhund Clubs of America, 3704 Lemoy Ferry Rd., St. Louis, MO 63125.

An Australian Shepherd Sled Dog Team

Owner: Steve Spencer

Spencer started in Australian Shepherds in the early 1980's and soon got into herding competition. However, living in Fairbanks, Alaska, caused some problems, one of which is the extremely short summer season. Spencer found he was spending most of the summer getting his dogs into good physical condition so they could compete in herding competitions but by the time they were ready, he had little time to actually compete. However, at one trial he met a dog trainer whose dogs were in top condition and learned from their owner that she ran her herding dogs with her husky sled dog team during the winter.

That fall Spencer bought a sled, harnesses and a husky lead dog. He quickly found his Aussies to be enthusiastic sled dogs, quickly learning the skills needed. After a couple years of running with the husky in lead, Spencer pulled the husky and ran an all Aussie team. In 1994, Spencer and his all Aussie team competed in their first competitive sled dog race and placed a very respectable fifth place. He said of the race, "It was quite an adventure! I wasn't sure how my Aussies would react to being passed by other teams. Fortunately, we only had one pass. I'm very happy with our fifth place finish!"

Search and Rescue

Search and rescue work is extremely rewarding. Certainly there is no value that can be put on a dog that finds a small child lost in the woods or an elderly person who wandered from a nursing home. Search and rescue dogs have worked the San Francisco, Mexico City, Armenian and Los Angeles earthquakes as well as flood emergencies, collapsed buildings and mudslides.

Search and rescue work does require a lot of training, sometimes as much as a year or two, depending upon the level of training you and your Aussie have prior to starting. You will need to know map reading, orienteering, wilderness survival, emergency first aid and much more. Your Aussie will need to learn how to use its nose, both for air scenting and tracking, and will need to be able to alert you when it has found a scent.

You and your Aussie both will have to be in good physical condition before you are able to search effectively. Your dog will need obedience training, and you must also have especially good off-leash control.

For more information, write: National Association for Search and Rescue, P.O. Box 3709, Fairfax, VA 22308, or: SAR Dog Alert, P.O. Box 39, Somerset, CA 95684.

Skijouring and Sledding

Skijouring has been around for centuries in Northern Europe and probably originated when a cross-country skier hooked up a reindeer and allowed the animal to pull him, providing the power. Horses have been used for skijouring for a number of years in both Europe and North America. It was only natural that eventually a dog would be used to pull: after all not everyone can keep reindeer, caribou or horses. Australian Shepherds can and have been used for skijouring; in fact, some of the dogs used by members of the Skijouring Club of Alaska are Australian Shepherds.

When people think of sled dog racing, they traditionally think of the Alaskan tundra and a half-frozen musher on a sled pulled by half-wild huskies traversing miles upon miles of frozen wasteland. Sled dog racing, however, can be for anyone with a sled and a team of dogs that like to run. Some of the different teams have even included Standard Poodles, Akitas, Irish Setters and German Shepherds. Australian Shepherds, with their natural athletic abilities and desire to work, do very well pulling although they cannot handle the extreme cold in some climates for an extended period of time.

For more information about skijouring and sledding, write: International Federation of Sled Dog Sports, 1763 Indian Valley Road, Novato, CA 94947. Or: International Sled Dog Racing Association, P.O. Box 446, Norman, ID 83848-0446.

Therapy Dogs

Ursa has an instinct for knowing who needs her and during visits to nursing homes or Alzheimer's care facilities, she will go directly to that person, sitting quietly by their side, nudging their hand until they pet her. She will allow kids to pull her ears, sit on her, climb all over her or cry into her coat. Her

Ursa and a new friend.

love and affection, given without reservation, have helped numerous people.

We, as dog owners, know that our dogs are good for us. They are good for us physically, mentally and emotionally. It has only been recently that researchers have come to the same conclusion, and out of this knowledge have emerged therapy dogs. Therapy dogs can help many people: the emotionally distraught, the mentally ill, abused children, orphaned or runaway kids, the sick, ill or elderly, the disabled or the lonely. Researchers

have not been able to pinpoint exactly why or how therapy dogs help people but they do have some guesses. First of all, therapy dogs provide love and affection without making demands; the dogs simply give love. The dogs are nonjudgemental; they do not care what people look like, how much money they have or what ethnic background they come from. And last, the dogs make people smile. Laughter is good for our soul and dogs love to make us laugh.

A therapy dog must be well-trained, with a good foundation in obedience training, especially sit, lay down and stay. The dogs cannot jump on people nor can they paw or scratch at people. During the specialized training for therapy dog work, the dog must be exposed to a variety of sights, sounds and smells that it will face in a nursing home, hospital or day-care center. These might include strollers, wheelchairs or gurneys, respirators, urine bags and diapers. The dog must be able to climb stairs, use an elevator and an escalator.

Many therapy dogs are taught specialized behaviors that can make their work easier, including putting the front feet up on the arm of a wheelchair or on the side of the bed and turning around so people in a chair or in bed can reach to pet it. Many therapy dog owners also teach their dog tricks to amuse the people they are visiting.

During the certification procedure, the dog must pass the AKC Canine Good Citizen test. For more information, write: Therapy Dogs International, 260 Fox Chase Rd., Chester, NJ 07930.

Tracking harnesses are adjustable to the size of your Aussie.

Tracking

Tracking is an activity that allows the dog to use its natural ability to smell. You can use tracking as a recreational sport, teaching your Aussie to "Go find Dad" or the kids; it can be used in search and rescue groups and can also be used as a sport. Both the AKC and ASCA offer two tracking titles—the Tracking Dog title, or TD, and the Tracking Dog Excellent, or TDX. To earn a tracking title from either the American Kennel Club or the Australian Shepherd Club of America your Aussie must be able to "Demonstrate its ability to recognize and follow human scent."

The Tracking Dog title requires your dog to follow a scented trail, which is called a "track," of four hundred forty to five hundred yards, making up to five right angle turns.

The track can be from thirty to one hundred-twenty minutes old. At the end of the "track" your Aussie is required to retrieve either your glove or wallet.

The Tracking Dog Excellent title requires your dog to follow a "track" of eight hundred to one thousand yards that is anywhere from three to five hours old. On this track your dog will make up to seven right angle turns, as well as demonstrate the ability to track through distractions and over "cross scents," which are scents laid over the original scented track. In both tests your Aussie is required to remain on a "long line" during the test.

For more information about tracking, ask your library or bookstore for, Tracking Dog, Theory and Methods by Glen Johnson, Arner Publications, NY. Or, Training the Competitive Working Dog, by Tom Rose and Gary Patterson, Giblaut Publishing, Company. Write to the AKC and ASCA for copies of the guidelines for tracking competition (Address for both organizations appear in Appendix A).

There Is So Much An Aussie Can Do!

The activities listed above are things that you and Aussie can do together, either for fun, for exercise or for competition. There are, however, some things Australian Shepherds can do if they can no longer remain in their original home.

U-CDX Sablue's Deja Vu CD, known to her friends as Susie, became a service dog after an obedience career and motherhood. Her original owner, Karin Wise, gave Susie to her friend, Karen True, when Karen was diagnosed with Multiple Sclerosis and needed help. Susie served her as a working partner and friend, even helping publicize the new organization Karin and Karen started, Working PAWS (Partners Able and Willing to Serve).

Robert Krause also lives a much fuller life because of an Aussie. Robert was injured in a diving accident and is now a quadriplegic. His partner, Kimba, retrieves household items identified by name, pulls his wheelchair and gives him ample love and affection, and has even protected him from an intruder. Robert calls Kimba his best friend.

Australian Shepherds are serving as guide dogs for the blind, hearing alert dogs for the hearing impaired and as with Susie and Kimba, service dogs for the disabled. Rescue groups or breeders that have promising dogs needing homes can contact training organizations that provide dogs for the disabled.

CHAPTER 9

Caring for Your Aussie

WHEN YOU TOOK your Aussie home, you assumed the responsibility of caring for it. Caring for it properly encompasses body and coat care, nutrition, exercise, play and training, as well as the dog's emotional well-being. All of these things require a commitment of time and effort from you but are amply rewarded by your Aussie's good health and, of course, its companionship.

The easiest way to make sure your dog is well cared for is to set up a routine and write it down, either on a sheet of paper posted on the refrigerator or on a bulletin board. If more than one person is involved in the dog's care, have people check off the items as they are completed. Once the routine is established, follow it. It is too easy to say, "Oh, I'll do that tomorrow" but this care is not something that can be procrastinated.

Daily Care Routine

Once a day, each and every day, you need to run your hands over your Aussie checking for ticks, burrs, foxtails, lumps, bumps, bruises, cuts and scrapes. As you do this each day, your fingers will get to know the feel of the dog and you will learn what feels normal and what does not. By checking the dog each day, you will be able to catch something before it turns into a much bigger problem.

The daily care massage contributes to your Aussie's physical and mental well-being. You will find that this becomes a special time for you and your Aussie.

During the massage run your hands down each leg, checking for possible cuts, injuries or burrs caught in the coat.

To do this, sit down on the floor and lay your Aussie on its side, and starting at the nose, run your hands over the muzzle and head. Get to know the shape of the head so you will be able to feel a bump or bruise or swollen lymph glands. Lift up your dog's lips and check its mouth. The gums should be firm; if they are swollen the dog might have some debris that needs to be cleaned out or there might be an infection. The eyes should be bright and clear with no discharge. Any dry matter, or "sleep," should be wiped away with a clean cotton ball.

Lift up each ear flap and check inside each ear. If the inside of the ear smells bad and there is a dark discharge or a build up of wax this may be an indication of infection. Run your fingers around each ear where it attaches to the head, sometimes ticks lodge themselves there. A tick will feel like a small to large bump under your fingers. If you find one, smear some Vaseline on it, thickly. The tick will not be able to breathe and will back out on its own. If it will not back out on its own, use tweezers to twist it out. Do not use your fingers to squish the tick or to pull it out. Lyme disease is spread by ticks, as are some other diseases, and you do not need to take the chance.

You might also find tangles of hair behind the ears or behind and between the back legs. Called mats, these can be combed out or very carefully trimmed out with rounded scissors. Mats can occasionally be found in the longer hair on the back legs, especially if a burr is in the hair and has started a tangle.

Continue your massage, working down your Aussie's neck and shoulders. Run your hands down each front leg, encircling the leg, checking the elbow for cuts and the armpit for ticks. Check the paw for burrs or foxtails lodged between the pads or cuts and scrapes. Burrs and foxtails can become imbedded, which is very painful, and can work themselves into the skin, causing an abscess.

Check each toenail. It is not necessary to trim the nails daily, but check the nail to make it has not broken. If it is rough or broken, you can trim it with a pair of nail clippers made for dogs or file it with an emery board or nail file. Do not use your nail clippers, as they will squeeze the nail and possibly split it.

After finishing the front feet, continue your examination of the dog's body, running your hands around the ribcage, down the back to the hips. Check the genital area. It is important you know what is normal and what is not, so if your Aussie has a genital discharge or swelling you will recognize the difference. Check the tummy, including the nipples. Feel for lumps or bumps.

Check for fleas. If fleas are a problem in your area and if your Aussie has any, you will see them on the tummy. To get rid of fleas, you need to get them off your Aussie by bathing or spraying it and by treating your house and the yard. Just doing one of the above will not do it. You will need to repeat the entire process, sometimes monthly throughout the summer. Fleas are survivors.

Continue your examination of your dog by checking its back legs and feet just as you did the front legs. Finish by checking its nub of a tail and the anal area. If the dog has had soft stools there might be evidence on its coat, in which case you will need to find out why. Did someone sneak the dog some scraps and upset its stomach?

Once you and your Aussie get the hang of this exam and you know what is normal and what is not, this will take you about ten minutes. Do not try to rush it. If you do, you may miss something important. Instead, take the time to do it thoroughly and spend at least ten minutes going over the dog. Then, once you have examined the dog, you can finish the exam by giving the dog a body massage. Your Aussie will totally relax and you both will enjoy it.

A side benefit of these daily examinations will show up when you need to take your Aussie to the veterinarian. Because your dog will be so used to being handled, if the veterinarian needs to look in the dog's ears or check its teeth, the exam will be easy and will not be as traumatic as if the dog was not handled thoroughly on a daily basis.

Exercise is part of the daily routine. The majority of behavior problems seen in young, healthy dogs are the result of too little exercise. Do you go for a walk? That is an outing, but it is not enough exercise for an Australian Shepherd. A young, healthy Aussie needs to work hard or vigorously run and play on a daily basis. If the dog is working stock, great, that is hard exercise. If the dog will play Frisbee, throw it until the dog reaches an anaerobic state, panting hard. Or take your dog running with you.

As with any exercise program, start it gradually and work up. Sore muscles are no fun for you or your dog. If your Aussie is a little older and has not been exercising regularly, have your veterinarian check it over before you start.

Feeding and Nutrition

TYPES OF DOG FOOD

Good nutrition is probably the single most important factor responsible for your Aussie's continued good physical and emotional health. A dog fed a poor food or a food it cannot adequately digest will have dull eyes, a poor coat, will lack energy and stamina and will not be able to work well. In addition, the dog may have food-related allergies and can, over time, develop other health problems including thyroid deficiencies, skin diseases, stomach and intestinal gas, rickets, bloat and a variety of other problems.

Dry food is recommended over canned dog foods because it has a good shelf life, is easily stored and provides good exercise for the teeth and gums. Canned foods are much more expensive and although they are very palatable to most dogs, they do not provide the good chewing action which can help keep the teeth clean. Semi-moist foods are also very palatable but many are preserved with sugar, an ingredient unneeded by most dogs, and like canned foods, do not provide any chewing exercise.

There are some very good dog foods on the market, the makers of which are conscientiously trying to produce a good, healthy product. Natural Life is a wonderful food with no chemical preservatives. Nature's Recipe offers a variety of foods, including a lamb and rice kibble with no by-products. Solid Gold is an all-natural kibble that is recommended for dogs with skin problems. Generations of dogs have grown up on Science Diet dog foods. Iams is another

brand that has been around for years and has a wonderful reputation.

There are also foods for every stage in the dog's life: puppy, adult, maintenance, gestation and lactation, performance, diet, senior, even foods for allergic or ill dogs. These foods vary by protein or fat content, ingredients, digestibility and more. Again, if you have questions about what food you should feed, call your veterinarian or the dog food manufacturer. Keep in mind while shopping and reading labels, as with many other things in life, cheaper is not necessarily better. The better quality dog foods will be more expensive.

INGREDIENTS

It is important that you know and understand what the label says and what is actually in the food you are feeding your Aussie. The label on the package of your dog's food will tell you, in decreasing order, the ingredients found in a particular food, as well as the protein, fat, fiber and water content.

Most dogs need meat in their diet. Scientifically classified as carnivores, meat is the mainstay of wild canines, although all will, if given the chance, eat fruits, berries and greens. Keep in mind, however, when a wild canine kills to eat, it usually eats the entire animal, including the skin and some of the fur, the entrails, the smaller bones, the marrow in the larger bones, the organs, even the food being digested in the intestinal tract.

The meat used in dog food does not have to meet the standards set for human consumption, which means just about any part of the animal can be included. An ingredient listed as "beef" does not mean ground round; it might be ears or muzzles, beef scraps or other cuts not fit for human consumption. An ingredient listed as "meat" or "meat meal" can be just about anything that comes off of an animal, including hide, hooves and meat scraps, and when listed as such, is usually a compilation of different kinds of animals. If it was only beef, it would be listed as "beef."

Beware of the phrase "by-products." If the label reads "chicken by-products," this does not mean scraps of chicken meat; it means heads, feet, bills, bones, even feathers. It can even mean waste products, diseased animals or tumors. Instead of feeding a food that lists "by-products" look for a food that lists a specific meat, such as beef, chicken or turkey.

Other ingredients that can add protein to the food might include dairy products, cheese, whey or eggs. This protein, whether from meat, eggs or dairy, is necessary for growth, for the development of strong muscles, bones and teeth, for healthy organs and coat and actually, for life itself. However, more is not better. Puppies need a higher protein content in their food (twenty-four to twenty-six percent is usually recommended) than adults. Dog foods are available with a protein content of over thirty percent, although, digesting and utilizing these diets can actually cause more harm than good. Consult your veterinarian about the correct protein content for your Aussie.

All dry kibble foods will also include a grain product, either wheat, soybeans, rice, barley or corn or a combination of several. These carbohydrates are comprised of starches, cellulose and sugar. The starches and sugars are sources of energy. The cellulose found in plants aids in the absorption of water and in the formation and elimination of stools.

Label-readers are used to looking at the fat content of food. We know we should reduce our fat intake, even though some fat is necessary, for us and for our dogs. Fat-soluble vitamins require fat to be used in the body. Fat helps maintain a healthy coat and alleviates dry skin and is also the most concentrated source of energy in times of hard work or stress. Fats also increase the palatability of food. Many of the dry dog foods advertised as "natural" foods use fats as a preservative. This can reduce the amount of chemicals contained in the food but often at a reduced shelf life. If you decide to feed your Aussie a dry food preserved with fat, make sure the food is not rancid when you buy it.

FOOD ALLERGIES

Food allergies, fortunately, are not common in Australian Shepherds. Some dogs scratch themselves raw if they eat wheat, while others have terrible intestinal gas if they eat soy. You might be able to identify food allergies simply by trial and error, but your veterinarian can administer an allergy test, similar to those used for identifying allergic reactions in humans. Once identified, it is often easy to eliminate the aggravating ingredients from your Aussie's diet.

THE FEEDING SCHEDULE

Any new food you choose should be introduced to your Aussie gradually. If you change over a period of three weeks, feeding 1/4 new food - 3/4 old food the first week, 1/2 new and 1/2 old the second week, and 3/4 new and 1/4 old the third week, your dog's system will have a chance to adjust. If you abruptly change foods, your dog will almost certainly have an upset stomach and diarrhea.

When your Aussie is a puppy, feed it two to three times a day, as much as it can or wants to eat in ten minutes. Then take the food away. As dogs grow up, most will, on their own, start eliminating one of the feeding times, maybe by just nibbling. By twelve to fourteen months of age, most dogs will be comfortable eating just once a day. Regulate how much to feed your dog by how it looks

and feels. If the dog is thin and acts hungry, give it more food. If the dog is fat, cut back. Along the same lines, if your dog has been working hard, give it extra food or if it has been sedentary, cut back.

When you feed your Aussie, do not leave food available to it all the time. Not only will this draw ants, squirrels and birds, your dog will think food is always available. It is more important that your dog learns that food comes from you. In a pack situation, the leader always eats first and gets the choicest food. In your family pack, you will always eat first and then you will feed your Aussie. When your dog is through, take away its bowl. If your dog plays with its food or walks away without finishing it after fifteen minutes, pick up the bowl anyway. Do not give your dog anything else to eat until it is time for the next meal.

HOMEMADE DOG FOODS

Some dog owners, frustrated over the quality of ingredients available in commercial dog foods, cook their own dog food. Other owners feel it is easier to control what their dog eats when they prepare the food. If your Aussie has a food allergy, feeding a homemade diet will make it easier to keep it away from foods that cause problems. If you do cook for your Aussie, you will need to take care it is being fed a quality, balanced diet. The following is a basic diet that would be suitable for most Australian Shepherds. Working dogs might need more, as would gestating or lactating bitches. A sedentary house dog would need less.

Cook one and a third cups of raw, white rice. Mix with one cup browned meat (ground beef, ground chicken or turkey, with grease drained off), a half cup chopped vegetables (carrots, green beans, peas, broccoli, and/or corn, cooked or raw) plus two tablespoons bone meal, a dash of iodized salt, a teaspoon vegetable oil and a heaping tablespoon active, live culture yogurt. Top it off with a good vitamin and mineral supplement, just as you would do with a commercial dog food.

You can vary this diet by replacing the rice with boiled or baked potatoes, by adding lentils or cooked kidney beans in place of the other vegetables, or by using cooked eggs or cheese in place of part of the meat. Keep in mind no one food is nutritionally complete, and where hamburger and rice with supplements are acceptable for a few meals, a deficiency may occur over a period of time. It is important when cooking a homemade diet that you pay particular attention to supplying your Aussie with a balanced diet, varying the ingredients, and paying close attention to your Aussie's health. At the first sign of a dull coat, excessive shedding, poor stools or any other change in the dog's health, talk to your veterinarian.

SUPPLEMENTS

Most experts agree a good quality commercial dog food contains, nutritionally, everything a dog needs. However, most dog owners add supplements to the food, for a variety of reasons. Some dog food manufacturers recommend that supplementation of their food not exceed ten percent of the quantity of food being fed, so that the nutritional components of their food remains in balance.

Many dog owners add yogurt to their dog's food. Yogurt has been said to aid digestion by adding beneficial bacteria to the intestinal tract. Yogurt is nutritious, a good source of fat, and certainly will not hurt the dog as long as your Aussie has no allergies to dairy products.

Brewer's yeast is another common supplement. Many dog owners believe dogs that eat brewer's yeast will naturally repel fleas. This has never been proven, though many dog owners adamantly believe in it. As with yogurt, yeast is an excellent food, providing B vitamins, and will not hurt the dog when used as a supplement.

Some dog owners give their dogs a multi-vitamin and mineral supplement. Again, this will not hurt the dog as long as it is given according to directions, but more is not better. Too much calcium can cause serious problems in puppies and growing dogs, as can zinc. Although water-soluble vitamins, like vitamin C, can be excreted through the urine, fat-soluble vitamins, such as A, will build up in the body and can actually become poisonous if oversupplemented.

Vitamin C has often been heralded as a wonder drug for people, fighting colds and boosting the immune system and just about as many claims have been made in behalf of Vitamin C for dogs. Some people swear it will prevent hip dysplasia or will at least help the symptoms if the dog already has it. Others say it will alleviate the symptoms of arthritis in an old dog. Scientifically, most of these claims are unproven; however, many dog owners supplement with Vitamin C on a daily basis, saying it will not hurt their dogs and could possibly help them.

Vegetables, vegetable juice or meat broth can be added to your Aussie's dry food. The vegetables add nutrition while the broth can make a dry food more palatable. Cooked eggs can be added as a nutritional supplement or to make the dry food more attractive, as can cheese or cottage cheese. A carrot makes a good chew treat and a slice of apple is a much better sweet treat than a commercial treat containing sugar and artificial colors.

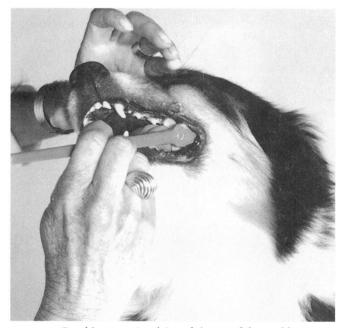

Brushing your Aussie's teeth is part of the weekly care routine.

Water

Water is necessary for life and your dog should always have access to fresh, clean water. Although drinking out of the toilet seems to be natural for many dogs, this should not be permitted, especially if you have a dye and scented cleaner installed that releases a small amount of chemical each time the toilet is flushed; many of these cleaners are toxic.

Eliminations

Your Aussie must have ample time to go outside to relieve itself. As an adult, your dog will probably have one to two bowel movements per day. During puppyhood, it may have several. The bowel movement should be solid and firm enough to hold together. A soft stool could be caused by diet, medications, stress or disease. If your Aussie has a stool that contains mucus or has blood in it, or a worm segment, save a piece of the stool in a plastic bag and call your veterinarian. Pick up your Aussie's feces daily. Accumulated stools will help spread disease or parasites, will smell, and will attract flies.

Your Aussie will also urinate several times a day. The frequency will depend upon how much the dog drinks, the size of its bladder and its individual preference. If the urine appears very dark in color, smells especially strong or appears to have blood in it, call your veterinarian right away.

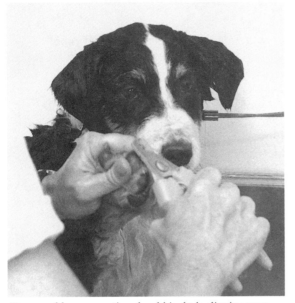

Your weekly care routine should include clipping your Aussie's nails.

Weekly Care

TEETH

Once a week, during your daily care routine, you need to clean your Aussie's teeth. There are several different ways to do this and many products on the market to help you. One of the easiest ways to keep your Aussie's teeth healthy, clean and looking good is to use gauze and baking soda. Wrap a couple of layers of wet gauze around your index finger, dip it into some baking soda and rub it back and forth over your dog's teeth. Use the baking soda liberally and let it sit on the dog's teeth for a few minutes before allowing the dog to drink. The baking soda will help guard against plaque build-up and if your Aussie eats dry food and regularly chews on rawhides or hard toys, its teeth should remain healthy longer.

If your Aussie already has some plaque built up, you may need help from your veterinarian to clean it off, then you can keep up on the routine care.

TOENAILS

Many active dogs will wear their toenails down, but if your Aussie runs on dirt or grass, its nails may need to be trimmed. Long nails are more than simply unsightly, they can actually deform the foot, arching the toes unnaturally and causing pain.

If your Aussie has any white nails, you can see the pink quick and you will be able to trim the nails without causing the quick to bleed. If your Aussie's nails are black, you can usually trim the hook at the end without trouble. If you are uncertain, use a nail file to file the nails shorter, and ask a dog groomer or your veterinarian to show you how to safely trim the nails. An alternative to clipping or hand filing nails is the use of a cordless rotary tool with a sandpaper bit. Even at low speeds, the rotary tool swiftly grinds back the nail. If you can train your Aussie to accept the disquieting sound of the motor, you will find that this is the easiest, fastest and safest way to keep nails short and properly shaped.

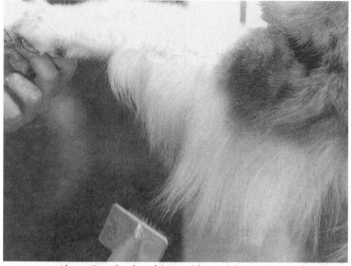

Above, Regular brushing, with special attention to the feathers, pants and behind the ears, will remove debris from the coat and prevent matting.
Below, To avoid mats, the hair around and between the toes should be trimmed on a regular basis.

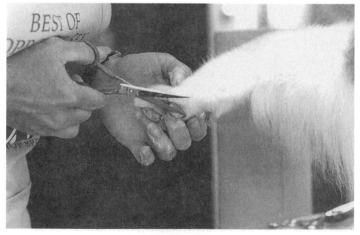

EARS

Once a week, gently wipe the inside of your Aussie's ears, using a cotton ball moistened with either alcohol, witch hazel or a product made especially for cleaning the ears. Clean only where your finger can easily move. Do not put your finger or a cotton swab into the ear canal.

A healthy ear will smell slightly damp and may have some dirt and wax residue but will not need more than one or two cotton balls to clean it out. If the ear smells bad (foul or dirty) and it takes several cotton balls to clean it, then it is time to call your veterinarian. If your Aussie is shaking its head a lot or is holding its head to one side, or is pawing or scratching at its ears, it may have a foxtail in its ear or mites or the start of an infection. Ear problems can sometimes be difficult to clear up and are very painful so do not procrastinate getting your Aussie in to see the veterinarian.

Coat Care

Australian Shepherds have a coat that is very easy to take care of. Many Aussie fanciers call the coat "wash and wear" because you can wash the dog, let it shake out and it is just about ready to go. Actually, your Aussie's coat needs more care than that, but not much more.

If you check your dog's body daily for burrs and foxtails, it can get by with one thorough brushing a week, although two or three times a week is better, especially in the spring and fall when the dog is shedding. You may want to lay your Aussie down on the floor to brush it, as you do when you check over its body and massage it. Start brushing at the head, working through the ruff (around the neck), brushing in the direction the coat grows. If you part the coat with one hand and brush with the other, you can get through the thickest coat. A wire or stiff bristle brush will help you get through the coat to the skin. Work around the neck and down to the shoulders, down the back, to the hips. Go back up to the neck and work down the chest, down the belly to the pantaloons (the hair on the back of the legs).

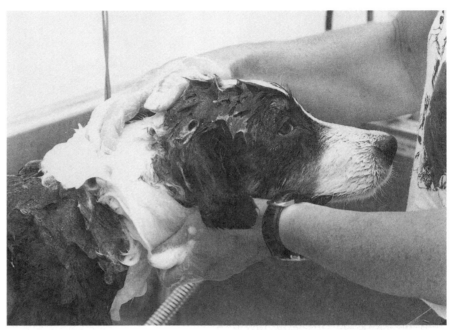

Regular bathing is an essential part of your Aussie's health care.

Then go back over your Aussie, brushing against the coat, loosening all the dead under-coat. Finish by running a comb over it in the direction the hair grows. When you are done, there should be no tangles and you should be able to run your fingers through the coat. It should feel soft to the touch.

If your Aussie is a working therapy dog, it will need to be bathed weekly or before each visit and because of this, you will need to use a very gentle shampoo that will not dry out the coat and skin. If your Aussie lives in the house at night and works hard on the farm during the day, it may need to be hosed off daily and shampooed every other week.

You will also want to keep the hair on its feet trimmed. Untrimmed hair on your dogs feet can mat and cause sores on the pads and will be more susceptible to foxtails becoming embedded. Use a pair of round tipped scissors and simply trim the hair between the pads and around the nails.

Yearly Vaccinations

Your Aussie's breeder probably started your dog on a vaccination schedule that you continued with your veterinarian. The commonly given vaccinations include: distemper, hepatitis, leptospirosis, parvovirus, corona virus and rabies. Depending upon where you live, your veterinarian might also recommend a Lyme disease vaccine. All of these diseases can rapidly kill unvaccinated puppies, even healthy adult dogs and occasionally, as with rabies, even people.

Vaccines are either killed or modified live forms of the actual virus. When injected, the vaccine stimulates your Aussie's immune system to produce antibodies so if your dog is exposed to the disease, its body will fight it off thus preventing illness. The creation of these vaccinations has saved millions of dogs' lives over the past few decades and it is vitally important that you keep track of your Aussie's vaccinations and get its yearly boosters. If you have any questions about which vaccines your Aussie should have and how often, ask your veterinarian.

Identifying Your Aussie

If your Aussie were to get out of your yard, do you have any means of making sure it would be returned to you? Is your dog specifically identifiable so that you could easily describe it to someone over the telephone. If there are three black tri-colored Australian Shepherds at your local Humane Society, how could you prove to the officer in charge which Aussie was yours?

The first means of identifying your Aussie is a collar and tags. The collar should be a buckle or quick release collar. Do not leave a choke or slip collar on your dog as it could get caught in a bush or on the fence, choke and kill your dog. The tags should include your

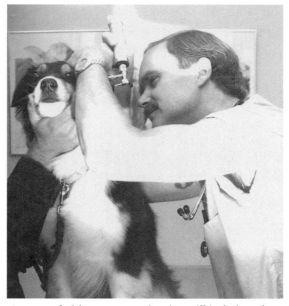

An annual visit to your veterinarian will include a physical examination, vaccinations and any other preventive care necessary.

dog's license, a rabies tag and an identification tag with your address and telephone number. When you go on vacation, let your dog wear a temporary tag with your hotel number or the campground written on it.

Although it is important your Aussie wear a buckle collar with identification tags, collars can come off. Your Aussie also needs permanent identification. A tattoo, usually placed on the inside of the right rear leg, can be a permanent identification. Most people use their Social Security number because it is a one-of-a-kind number. Other familiar numbers might include the dog's AKC or ASCA number, your driver's license number, or a spouse's birthday. The numbers used are not as important as the fact the numbers are registered with the National Dog Registry, an organization whose sole function is to maintain a list of dog tattoos and notifying owners when the dog has been found.

I can personally testify the system works. Several years ago my old dog, that was getting slightly senile, got out of our yard while my husband and I were at work. He was found about five miles away by a kind-hearted person who did not want to see him get hit by a car. When he rolled over to get his tummy rubbed, she saw his tattoo and called the local Humane Society, who called the National Dog Registry. They called me at work to tell me where my dog was before I even knew he was lost.

The National Dog Registry's telephone number is 914-679-2355. They also maintain a list of people who can tattoo your dog for you.

Emergency First Aid

It is often difficult for many dog owners to make a decision about when they need to call their veterinarian and when they can handle a dog's health problem at home. Listed below are some commonly seen problems and some basic advice about how you might handle them. However, the price of a telephone call to your veterinarian is small compared to your dog's life. When in doubt, call!

First, assess the problem. When you are trying to decide what is wrong with your Aussie, you will need to play detective, to put the puzzle pieces together. If you need to call

your veterinarian, you will also have to answer some questions. First of all, what does your Aussie look like? What was your first clue something was wrong? Is the dog eating normally? What do its stools look like? Is the dog limping? Where? Is any part of its body swollen or red? Is anything painful? Does the dog have a temperature? (Use a rectal thermometer. Normal is 101 to 102 degrees.) Write down all of these clues and be prepared to tell your veterinarian.

VOMITING

Did your Aussie vomit up anything? Was there a foreign body—pieces of sticks, or garbage? If there are no other symptoms, withhold food for twelve hours, and water for several hours. When vomiting has stopped, offer water in ice cube form or in small quantities. If the vomiting continues for more than twelve hours, call your veterinarian.

DIARRHEA

What did the stools look like? Was there mucus or blood? Was a foreign body in the stool. Have you changed your Aussie's food? This can cause diarrhea, especially if changed rapidly. Withhold food for twelve hours but do not withhold water, as diarrhea can cause dehydration. Many veterinarians advise owners to give Keopectate or Pepto Bismal for diarrhea. Call your veterinarian and ask his opinion, ask also what dosage you should give. If the diarrhea lasts for more than twelve hours, call your veterinarian and save a stool sample for him to examine. Persistent diarrhea can be symptomatic of very serious diseases.

OVERHEATING OR HEATSTROKE

Overheating is characterized by rapid or difficult breathing, vomiting, even collapse, and you need to act at once. Immediately place your Aussie in a tub of cold water or if a tub is not available, run water from a hose over your dog. Use a rectal thermometer to take its temperature and call your veterinarian immediately. If ice is available, place an ice pack on your Aussie's head and stomach. Encourage your dog to drink some of the cool water. Transport the dog to your veterinarian as soon as possible.

FRACTURES

Because your Aussie will be in great pain, you should muzzle it, using a soft cloth or a pair of pantyhose. (Wrap the pantyhose around its muzzle and then tie it behind its head.) Do not attempt to set the fracture but try to immobilize it, if possible, by splinting it with a piece of wood and then wrapping it with gauze or another pair of pantyhose. If there is a board or a door you can use as a backboard or a stretcher so the injured limb is stable, do it. Transport your Aussie to your veterinarian as soon as you can, moving the dog as little as possible.

SNAKEBITE

Without inviting danger, try to look at the snake, making note of colors, markings, and patterns so you or your veterinarian can identify the species. In many instances a dog is bitten by a poisonous snake that did not inject venom. In these cases, no serious symptoms develop and cleaning the wound with hydrogen peroxide is sufficient treatment. If you know your Aussie has been bitten by a poisonous snake or it exhibits symptoms that include pain, swelling, salivation, vomiting, labored breathing and convulsions, keep it as quiet as possible to restrict the spread of venom. If the bite is on a limb apply a loose tourniquet above the wound (you should be able to easily insert a finger beneath the tourniquet). An icepack should be applied to the swelling. If your Aussie is in pain or is frantic, muzzle it. Call your veterinarian as soon as possible.

POISONING

Symptoms of poisoning include retching and vomiting, diarrhea, salivation, labored breathing, dilated pupils, weakness, collapse or convulsions. Sometimes one or more symptoms will appear, depending upon what was ingested or inhaled. If you suspect your Aussie has been in contact with something poisonous, time is critical. Call your veterinarian immediately. If your veterinarian is not immediately available, call the Animal Poison Hotline at 1-800-548-2423. The hotline and your veterinarian will need to know what your dog ingested and how much. Do not make your Aussie vomit unless instructed to do so.

ANIMAL BITES

Muzzle your Aussie if it is in pain. Trim the hair from around the wound and then liberally pour hydrogen peroxide over it. A hand-held pressure bandage can help stop the bleeding. Call your veterinarian as soon as possible as he may want to see it. Stitches may be necessary if the bite is a rip or gash and putting your Aussie on antibiotics may be recommended.

BLEEDING

Again, if your Aussie is in pain, muzzle it. Place a gauze pad, or, if that is not available, a clean terry cloth towel, over the wound and apply pressure. If the wound is deep and could require stitches, or if bleeding does not stop, call your veterinarian immediately. If the wound is on a leg and continues to bleed, a soft tourniquet can be applied but make sure it is loosened every three to five minutes.

CHOKING

If your Aussie is pawing at its mouth, gagging, coughing, drooling or has collapsed, immediately open its mouth and look down its throat. If an object is visible, pull it out, using your fingers, tweezers or a pair of pliers. If you cannot see the object or cannot pull it out, hit your Aussie behind the neck or between the shoulders to try and dislodge it. If this fails, try a Heimlich maneuver, adapted for dogs. Grasp either side of Aussie's ribcage and apply quick, firm pressure. Repeat.

If your Aussie can get some air around the obstruction, get it to your veterinarian as soon as possible. If your Aussie cannot get air around the obstruction, you do not have time to move the dog. Work on getting the object out of its throat.

DROWNING

If possible, hold up your Aussie by the hind legs to allow the water to drain from the trachea and lungs. Set the dog down on its side with the tail end higher than the head. Make sure the tongue is pulled well forward and there is no foreign matter obstructing the airway. Press and release the ribcage with a flat hand steadily and rhythmically at two-second intervals.

Water should run from the mouth and when this stops turn the dog on its other side and repeat the process. The dog should be dried and kept warm.

WHEN IN DOUBT

You are responsible for your Aussie's well-being, so whenever you are in doubt as to how to care for it, call. A groomer will be a professional more than happy to talk to you about coat care, brushes, matts, flea control or toenail clipping. Your veterinarian will talk to you about emergency first aid, food, ear and teeth cleaning and anything else that might come up. The dog food manufacturer will talk to you about food ingredients, quality control, food amounts needed and different kinds of food. After all, the more you know about your Aussie and its care, the better you can take care of your dog.

CHAPTER 10

The Health of Your Aussie

THE BEST SAFEGUARD for your Aussie's health is to develop a working relationship with a veterinarian that you trust. Talk to him or her about your dog, its health, activity level, its parents and genetic heritage, your dog's breeder, and then listen to your veterinarian's responses. And ask questions. If your veterinarian is threatened by your questions, find another veterinarian. Your Aussie is your dog, your companion and it is up to you to make sure it lives a long, healthy, happy life.

External Parasites

FLEAS

A flea is a small insect, about the size of the head of a pin. It is crescent-shaped, has six legs and is a tremendous jumper. Fleas live by biting the host animal and ingesting its blood

You can tell if your Aussie has fleas by back-brushing its coat and looking at the skin. A flea will appear as a tiny darting speck, trying to hide in the hair. Roll your Aussie over and check its belly near the genitals; the fleas will be scurrying to hide. You can also tell by laying your dog on a solid-colored sheet and brushing vigorously. If you see salt and pepper type of residue falling onto the sheet, your Aussie has fleas. The residue is made up of fecal matter (the "pepper") and flea eggs (the "salt").

Great survivors, flea eggs can live in the environment for years waiting for the right conditions to hatch; this is not an insect that can be ignored. A heavy infestation of fleas can actually kill an animal, bleeding it dry. Keep in mind each time a flea bites, it eats a drop of blood. Multiply that by several bites a day (or more) times the number of fleas on the animal.

The flea, biting its host, can also cause innumerable skin problems. Many dogs develop flea allergy dermatitis, a reaction to the flea bite. The bite causes a never ending cycle of self destruction: the flea bites, the skin itches, the dog scratches or chews in response, the skin becomes even more irritated, so the dog bites or chews even more. Soon, the dog is miserable and needs veterinary care.

Fleas can also carry disease. Rats and fleas were the carriers of the bubonic plague in Europe and Asia during the time of the Black Plague. Fleas are also the intermediary host for tapeworms. If you have found small, rice-like segments near your dog's rectum or in its stools, your dog has tapeworms.

To reduce the flea population, you need to treat the dog and the environment. If you simply treat your Aussie, and do not treat the yard, house or car, your dog will become reinfected. If your Aussie is working on a ranch and it is not possible (or desirable) to constantly use insecticides, then you will have to concentrate on keeping the dog itself flea-free.

There are a number of different products on the market, including both strong chemical insecticides and natural botanical products. What you decide to use depends upon how bad your flea problem is, and your preferences. The stronger chemicals, such as organophosphates and carbamates, will kill the fleas, of course, but they can also kill local birds and wildlife. You must take care that you use them properly.

The natural products are not as strong and some of them do not kill the insect immediately, sometimes it takes a few hours. Some of the natural products (like Bioflea Halt) use silica or diatomaceous earth to cut or erode the flea's shell so that it dehydrates. There are also natural products that use citrus oils, eucalyptus or pennyroyal oils to repel fleas.

If you have questions about the ingredients or use of a particular product, call the manufacturer. They will be more than willing to talk with you and explain exactly how it should be used.

TICKS

Ticks are another parasite that cannot be ignored. There are several different kinds of ticks; all are roundish insects that bury their head in the skin of the host animal. They feed on the host's blood and when full and engorged, drop off.

Unfortunately, ticks can be very dangerous and can carry several potentially deadly diseases. Rocky Mountain spotted fever is carried by the infectious agent Rickettsia rickettsii, a parasite. Dogs that get Rocky Mountain Spotted Fever (RMSF) run a temperature of 104 degrees or higher, become listless and depressed, do not eat, have swollen lymph glands and often have difficulty breathing. When people get RMSF, the symptoms include fever, headache and a rash. RMSF can be accurately diagnosed by a blood test and antibiotic treatment is required to clear it up.

Lyme disease was first reported in Lyme, Connecticut, but has now spread and can be found in most areas of the country. It is caused by a spirochete-type of bacteria most commonly spread through people and animals by the deer tick (ixodes dammini) although it has been reported in other ticks as well.

In dogs, Lyme disease causes arthritis-type symptoms and lameness, fever, loss of appetite, lymph node enlargement and kidney disease. In people, Lyme disease first appears with a rash which looks like a bull's eye and is considered a sure identification of Lyme disease. If untreated, the disease progresses and is normally characterized by heart problems, arthritis-type symptoms, especially in the knees, wrists and ankles. Most cases of Lyme disease respond well to antibiotic treatment, although treatment may take months to complete.

Tick paralysis is more commonly seen in dogs than it is in people, although it can also affect humans. Tick paralysis occurs when a female tick attaches to the dog and begins to

Companionship and affection are as important to the health of your Aussie as food and shelter.

feed. She injects a neurotoxin, which causes paralysis that progresses over time, usually seven to nine days. If the tick is removed, paralysis fades fairly rapidly; however, if the tick is not found and remains on the dog, death can result from respiratory paralysis.

While some flea product manufacturers claim through advertising that their products kill ticks, it is always best to be sure your Aussie is tick free by examining it on a daily basis during tick season. If you run your hands over your dog every day (especially after an off-lead outing), covering every inch of its body, you will find any embedded ticks on your dog. They will feel like a small bump under your fingers. Smear a thick coating of Vaseline over the tick and grab it with a piece of paper towel or toilet paper as it backs out of the skin. If the tick does not back out, use a pair of tweezers to gently pull it out of the skin. Look at it to make sure the head is attached. If the head has broken off and is still in the skin, an infection or abscess may result. Never use your fingers to remove a tick; the dangers of disease transmission are too great. Kill the tick by dropping it in alcohol for a few minutes and then flushing it down the toilet. Do not flush a live tick—it will survive.

Internal Parasites

ROUNDWORMS

These long, white worms (toxocara canis) are common internal parasites, especially in puppies, although they are occasionally found in adult dogs and people. The adult female roundworm can lay up to two hundred thousand eggs a day, which are passed out in the dog's feces. Roundworms can only be transmitted via the feces. Because of this, stools should be picked up daily, and your Aussie should be prevented from investigating other dogs' feces.

If dealt with early, roundworms in adult dogs are not serious, however, a heavy infestation can severely effect a dog's health. Puppies with roundworms will not thrive and will appear thin, with a dull coat and a pot-bellied appearance. In people, roundworms can be more serious. Therefore early treatment, regular fecal checks and good sanitation are important, both for your Aussie's continued good health and yours.

HOOKWORMS

Hookworms (unicinaria and ancylostoma) live their adult lives in the small intestines of dogs. They attach to the intestinal wall and suck blood. When they detach and move to a new location, the old wound continues to bleed because of the anticoagulant the worm injects when it bites. Bloody diarrhea is usually the first sign of a problem.

Hookworm eggs are passed through the feces and are either picked up from stools, as with roundworms, or if conditions are right, hatch in the soil and attach themselves to the feet of their new hosts where they then burrow into the skin. After burrowing through the skin, they migrate to the intestinal tract, where the cycle starts all over again.

People can pick up hookworms, too, often by walking barefoot in infected soil. In the Sunbelt states, children often pick up hookworm eggs when playing outside in the dirt or in a sandbox. Treatment, for both dogs and people, may have to be repeated.

TAPEWORMS

Tapeworms attach to the intestinal wall to absorb nutrients. They grow by creating new segments and usually the first sign of an infestation is when you see rice-like segments in your Aussie's stool or on its coat near the rectum. Tapeworms are acquired when the dog eats an intermediate host; the most common host is the flea. Therefore, a good flea control program is the best way to prevent a tapeworm infestation.

WHIPWORMS

Adult whipworms live in the large intestine where they feed on blood. The eggs are passed in the stool and can live in the soil for many years. If your Aussie eats fresh spring grass, or buries its bone in the dirt, it can pick up eggs from infected soil. If you garden, you can pick up eggs under your fingernails, infecting yourself when you touch your face.

Heavy infestations cause diarrhea, often watery or bloody. The dog may appear thin and anemic, with a poor coat. Severe bowel problems may result from an infestation. Unfortunately, whipworms can be difficult to detect as the worms do not continually shed eggs. Therefore, a stool sample collected on any given day may be clear, while one collected the next day may show eggs. In other words a negative stool sample does not mean your Aussie does not have whipworms, it simply means no eggs were present in that sample.

GIARDIA

Giardia is a bacterial infection common in wild animals which lives in the mucous membrane of the small intestine. It is transmitted from one animal to another through drinking water contaminated with the bacteria. The dangers of giardia infection are serious for both you and your dog. So if you take your Aussie camping or hiking be aware that free standing water, lakes and streams are a likely source for this disease. Diarrhea is usually one of the first symptoms.

HEARTWORM

Adult heartworms live in the upper heart and greater pulmonary arteries where they damage the vessel walls. Poor circulation results, which in turn causes damage to other bodily functions and eventually death is caused by heart failure.

The adult worms produce thousands of tiny larvae called microfilaria. These circulate throughout the bloodstream until they are sucked up by the intermediary host, a mosquito. The microfilaria goes through the larval stages in the mosquito, then it is transferred to another dog when the mosquito bites again.

Dogs infected with heartworms can be treated if the infestation is diagnosed early. The good news is that there are effective medications available that prevent heartworm. Usually a blood test is analyzed and if the results are negative preventive medication is given. Since heartworm is endemic in many parts of the United States, prevention is the wisest choice for your Aussie.

Infectious Diseases

The diseases listed below can all be prevented by vaccinations, but vaccinating your Aussie as a puppy is no guarantee that it will not get sick. There are many factors that govern how a dog reacts to a vaccination, including the antibodies the puppy got from its mother, how the dog's own immune system reacts to the vaccine and its general state of health. Set up a vaccination schedule with your veterinarian and stick to it, making sure your Aussie completes its puppy shots and gets its yearly boosters.

DISTEMPER

Distemper is a contagious viral disease which used to kill thousands of dogs. With the advent of new, effective vaccinations, it should not kill any dogs today, but still does. Dogs with distemper have a fever, are weak and depressed, have a discharge from the eyes and nose, cough, vomit and have diarrhea. An infected dog sheds viruses in the saliva, urine and feces. Intravenous fluids and anti-biotics may help support an infected dog but, unfortunately, most infected dogs die.

A distemper vaccination can normally prevent distemper, however, vaccines work by stimulating the immune system. If there is a problem with the immune system or if your Aussie has not received a complete series of vaccinations, it may not be adequately protected.

HEPATITIS

Infectious canine hepatitis is a highly contagious virus that primarily attacks the liver but can also cause severe kidney damage. It is not related to the form of hepatitis that affects people. The virus is spread through contaminated saliva, mucus, urine or feces. Initial symptoms include depression, vomiting, abdominal pain, high fever and jaundice. Mild cases may be treated with intravenous fluids, antibiotics and even blood transfusions, however, the mortality rate is very high. Vaccinations, usually combined with the distemper vaccine, can prevent hepatitis.

CORONAVIRUS

Coronavirus is a virus that is rarely fatal to adult dogs although it is frequently fatal to puppies. The symptoms include vomiting, loss of appetite and a yellowish, watery stool that might contain mucus or blood. The stools carry the shed virus, which is highly contagious.

Fluid or electrolyte therapy can alleviate the dehydration associated with diarrhea, but there is no treatment for the virus itself. There is a vaccine available, sometimes given alone, sometimes given with the distemper, hepatitis, leptospirosis and parvo vaccinations.

PARVOVIRUS

Parvovirus, or parvo as it is commonly known, is a terrible killer of puppies. A severe gastrointestinal virus, parvo attacks the inner lining of the intestines, causing bloody diarrhea with a very distinctive odor. In puppies under ten weeks of age, the virus attacks the heart, causing death, often with no other symptoms.

The gastroenteritis can be treated with fluid therapy and antibiotics, however, the virus moves rapidly and dehydration can lead to shock and death in a matter of hours. There is a vaccination for parvo, which is often given combined with the distemper, hepatitis, leptospirosis and corona vaccines.

LEPTOSPIROSIS

Leptospirosis is a bacterial disease, rather than a virus. The disease is spread by infected wildlife; the bacteria being shed in the urine. When your Aussie sniffs at a bush that has been urinated on, or drinks from a contami-nated stream, it may pick up the bacteria. The bacteria then attacks the kidneys, causing kidney failure. Unfortunately, people can also pick up leptospirosis.

Symptoms of lepto include: fever, loss of appetite, possible diarrhea and jaundice. Antibiotics can be used to treat the disease but the outcome is usually not good, due to the serious kidney and liver damage caused by the bacteria. Consideration must also be taken with the highly contagious aspects of the disease; to other dogs, animals and people. Dogs do receive a vaccination for lepto, usually included with the distemper, hepatitis, parvo and corona vaccines.

TRACHEOBRONCHITIS

Commonly called kennel cough or canine cough, this respiratory infection can be caused by any number of different viral or bacterial agents. These highly contagious, airborne agents can cause a variety of symptoms, including inflammation of the trachea, bronchi and lungs as well as mild to severe coughing. Antibiotics may be prescribed to combat or prevent pneumonia and a cough suppressant may quiet the cough.

Some forms of the disease may be prevented by vaccination, such as bordetella bronchiseptica and canine adenovirus, but there are so many causes, vaccinations alone cannot prevent tracheobronchitis.

RABIES

Rabies is a highly infectious virus usually carried by wildlife, especially by bats, raccoons and skunks, although any warm blooded animal, including people, may become infected. The virus is transmitted in saliva through a bite or break in the skin.

The virus then travels up to the brain and spinal cord and throughout the body.

Behavior changes are the first symptom of rabies. Nocturnal animals come out during the day, fearful or shy animals become bold and aggressive, or friendly and affectionate. As the disease progresses, the animal will have

trouble swallowing and will drool or salivate excessively because of nerve paralysis. As the disease progresses, paralysis and convulsions develop. Although there is no effective treatment for rabies, vaccinations which prevent transmission of the virus have been available for many years.

Eyes and Ears

Unfortunately, the Australian Shepherd is one of many breeds known to have eye defects. There are several different types of eye defects found, some are known, others are presently being researched. It is still unknown how many of the defects are genetically transmitted, although most are assumed to be hereditary. Researchers do think that the genes which cause eye defects are neither simple dominant or recessives. It seems that multiple genes and modifiers might play a part in different defects.

Australian Shepherds should have an eye screening as early as eight weeks of age, prior to being sold or going to new homes. Every Aussie, especially those used in a breeding program, should have its eyes examined every year. The examination should be performed by a Veterinary Ophthalmologist, certified by the American College of Veterinary Ophthalmologists (AVCO).

Once examined and shown to be free of eye disease, the ophthalmologist can send the results in to the Canine Eye Registry Foundation (CERF). CERF has established a veterinary medical data bank that is used for researching trends in eye defects and breed susceptibility. CERF's goal is to eliminate heritable eye disease in purebred dogs through registration, research and education. CERF welcomes inquiries from breeders wishing to make sure that their stock is disease-free or from dog fanciers needing more information. CERF's telephone number is 317-494-8179.

HOMOZYGOUS MERLE EYE DEFECT

The beautiful merle coloring so many people enjoy in the Australian Shepherd (and in some other breeds as well) has a hidden agenda. How the gene which produces the merle coloring also affects eye and ear development in the fetus is unknown. When a merle bitch is bred to a merle dog, the odds are that one out of every four puppies produced will have either an eye or hearing defect. That is a big responsibility breeders must take into consideration.

Some of the defects found include: micropthalmia (abnormally small eyes), sub-luxated pupils (pupils that are off center in the iris), iris colobomas (holes or abnormal openings in the iris), optic disc colobomas (irregularities in the optic disc), retinal dysplasia (folded or detached retinas), persistent puliary membrane (a fetal covering of the pupil which fails to disappear by five weeks of age), and cataracts (opacities on the lens). These defects are often flagged (or accompanied) by excess white markings on the puppy's head.

COLLIE EYE ANOMALY

Collie eye anomaly may or may not affect a dog's vision. While it is hereditary, possibly a simple recessive, and is present at birth and remains the same throughout the dog's life. The Aussie suffering from collie eye anomaly will have the following conditions: staphlomas (a bulging of the rear wall of the eyeball), optic disc coloboma (irregularities in the optic disc), retinal dysplasia (folded or detached retinas), and choroid hypoplasia (incomplete development of the blood vessels in the back of the eye).

The Australian Shepherd Club of America recommends that every puppy in every litter be checked for collie eye anomaly before four months of age. As the dog matures, the natural pigmentation in the back of the eye makes it more difficult to detect. Any dog showing signs of collie eye anomaly, or any dog from a litter with a positive diagnosis, should be spayed or neutered and removed from any breeding plans.

PROGRESSIVE RETINAL ATROPHY

Progressive retinal atrophy (PRA) is the progressive degeneration of the retina. The retinal light receptor cells in the eye gradually atrophy; this, combined with the progressive reduction in size of the retinal blood vessels which nourish the eye, causes gradually blindness. Signs of the disease normally begin anywhere between eight weeks and six months of age, although it can start showing up later, even as late as six or seven years of age. As the retina deteriorates, the dog gradually loses vision until it is totally blind.

Most experts agree that PRA is carried on a recessive gene. Although many breeds have serious problems with PRA, Australian Shepherds, luckily, are not among them. Since PRA has occurred in the breed, all dogs should be routinely screened prior to breeding. Any dog showing signs of PRA, or any dog from a litter with a positive diagnosis, should be spayed or neutered.

HYLOID ARTERIES

Hyloid arteries are small blood vessels that extend from the optic disc to the lens before birth, normally to disappear by or shortly after birth. Sometimes all or part of them remain, sometimes functional and carrying blood. The presence of a hyloid artery is associated with opacities of the lens. It is unknown how hyloid arteries are passed, or even whether or not they are hereditary. Because they are associated with opacities of the lens and a decrease in vision, dogs with hyloid arteries should not be used in a breeding program.

DEAFNESS

Deafness is associated with the white color gene. In Australian Shepherds, dogs resulting from the breeding of two merles—a merle bitch and a merle dog—have a twenty-five percent chance of vision or hearing defects; that's one out of four puppies. These dogs usually have white on the head, around the eyes and ears. Many breeders make the difficult decision to cull, or kill, at birth those puppies with excessive white. Because of these odds, experts in the breed recommend that merles be bred only to solid or tri-colored dogs.

Hip Dysplasia

Hip dysplasia (HD) is a disease of the coxofemoral joint; to put it simply, it is a failure of the head of the femur (thigh bone) to properly fit into the acetabulum (hip socket). HD is not simply caused by poorly formed or positioned bones; many researchers, including Gail Smith, D.V.M., Ph.D., an Associate Professor in the Department of Clinical Studies at the University of Pennsylvania School of Veterinary Medicine,

The aging Aussie needs additional special care.

believe that the muscles and tendons in the leg and hip may also play a part in the disease. HD is considered to be a polygenic inherited disorder, which means that many factors come into play. Many different genes may lead to the disease, not just one. Also, environmental factors may lead to HD, including nutrition and exercise, although the part that environmental factors play in the disease is highly debated among experts.

HD can cause a wide range of problems, from mild lameness to movement irregularities to crippling pain. Dogs with HD must often limit their activities, may need corrective surgery or may even need to be euthanized because of the pain.

Contrary to popular belief, HD cannot be diagnosed by watching a dog run or by the way it lays down; HD can be diagnosed accurately only by x-ray. Once the x-ray is taken, it can be sent to the Orthopedic Foundation of America (OFA, University of Missouri, Columbia, MO 65211), which grades and certifies the x-rays of dogs over the age of two years. Sound hips are rated excellent, good or fair and the dog's owner will receive a certificate with the rating. A dysplastic dog will be rated as mild, moderate or severe. A dog that has been found to be dysplastic should be spayed or neutered.

Bloat

Bloat is the acute dilation of the stomach, caused when the stomach fills with gas and air, and swells. This swelling prevents the dog from vomiting or passing gas, and as a result, the pressure builds, cutting off blood from the heart and to other parts of the body. This causes shock or heart failure, both of which can cause death. Bloat can also cause torsion, where the stomach turns or twists on its long axis, again causing shock and death.

The first symptoms of bloat are obvious. The dog will be pacing and panting, showing signs of distress. The dog's sides will begin to distend. To be successful, treatment should begin at once—there is no time to fool around. If the pressure is not immediately relieved, death can follow within an hour.

Bloat is seen most often in large, deep-chested breeds but has been seen in Australian Shepherds. To prevent bloat, do not allow your Aussie to drink large quantities of water after exercising or after eating and limit exercise for a couple of hours after eating.

As Your Aussie Grows Older

Australian Shepherds live, on the average, fourteen years. However, to live that long, remaining healthy and happy, your dog will need your help. Aging in dogs, as in people, brings some problems. You will probably see your dog's vision dim, its hearing fade and joints stiffen. Heart and kidney disease are common in old dogs. Reflexes will not be as sharp as they were and your dog may be more sensitive to heat and cold. Your dog may also get grouchy, showing less tolerance to younger dogs, children and other things that are not part of its normal routine.

An old dog that has lived with you all its life is a special gift. Your old Aussie knows your ways, your likes and dislikes and your habits. It seems almost able to read your mind and its greatest joy is to be close to you. Your old Aussie may not be able to herd the cattle or sheep any more, or soar over the agility course, but it can still be a wonderful companion that needs your care to help it through its old age comfortably.

ARTHRITIS

Arthritis is common in most old dogs. Like many diseases, the causes have not been fully determined. It is known that there are three major classifications of arthritis in dogs: rheumatoid, osteoarthritis and septic. Septic arthritis is seen less often and caused by bacterial infection in the joints. Antibiotics are principally the effective treatment. More common is osteoarthritis, which causes a slow degeneration of bone surfaces in the joints of older dogs. Stiffness, pain and even crippling can result, and most afflicted dogs react poorly to cold weather or too much physical exertion. Rheumatoid arthritis is similar to the kind of arthritis affecting humans. The treatments for rheumatoid arthritis and osteoarthritis are similar: a draft-free, warm living environment, heating pads, cushioned sleeping pads, aspirin and, in extreme cases, injections of cortiscosteroids. Practitioners of natural healing claim success with anti-inflammatory herbs like yucca and feverfew. Among other successful techniques are food supplements containing amino acids and antioxidants.

NUTRITION

As your Aussie's activity level slows down, it will need to consume fewer calories and as its body ages, your dog will need less protein. However, your dog's body may be less able to process and digest the food it eats and this may show up in a poor coat or stools. A heaping tablespoon of active, live-culture yogurt can help digestion, plus several of the premium grade dog food manufacturers produce foods specially formulated for old dogs.

Ch. Brigadoon's California Dude CD, HI at ten years of age. He was Winners Dog and Best of Winners at the ASCA National Specialty, 1985.

TEETH

Your Aussie may need to have its teeth cleaned professionally and this is something that cannot be procrastinated. Bacteria that build up on the teeth, called plague, can infect the gums, get into the bloodstream and cause infections in other parts of the body, including the heart and kidneys.

EXERCISE

Exercise is still important to your Aussie. Your dog needs the stimulation of moving around and of seeing and smelling the world, although the exercise must be tailored to your Aussie's needs and abilities. If your dog can still chase the Frisbee, let it and if you know

that jumping causes pain, throw the Frisbee low and flat so that your dog can catch it without jumping.

If your Aussie is capable only of going for a walk, do that. Let your old dog set the pace and protect it from extremes of weather and stray dogs.

Herbal Remedies

If you use herbal or homeopathic remedies yourself, you may be interested in learning that many of these remedies are available for their dogs as well. Vitamin C is recommended for dogs with arthritis. Rose hips, also a good source of Vitamin C, aids the digestion, as does live-culture yogurt. Chamomile tea is calming and is good for an upset stomach. Yucca is a natural anti-inflammatory and is wonderful for aches and pains as well as arthritis. For more information, check at your library for books on herbal medicine. There are several available written just for dog care.

When It Is Time

We have the option, with our dogs, not to let them suffer when they are old, ill and infirm. There will come a time when you will need to decide when and how to end your Aussie's suffering . Some people feel that the time has come when the dog is no longer enjoying life, when it is incontinent and despondent because it has broken house-training or when the bad days outnumber the good days. Only you can make the decision to spare your Aussie the humiliation of incontinence, convulsions, or the inability to stand up or move.

If your old Aussie must be helped to its death, your veterinarian can give an injection that is an overdose of anesthetic. It will go to sleep and quietly stop breathing. Be there with your dog. Let your arms hold your old friend and let your dog hear your voice saying how much you love it as it goes to sleep. There will be no fear and the last thing your dog will remember is your love.

Grieving

A well-loved dog is an emotional invest-ment of unparalleled returns. Unfortunately, our dogs' lives are much too short and we must learn to cope with inevitable loss. Grief is a natural reaction to the loss of a loved one, whether it is a pet, a spouse, friend or a family member. Grief has no set pattern; its intensity and duration are different for each person and can be different for each loss.

Sometimes the best outlet for grief is a good hard cry. For other people talking about the pet or your loss is good therapy. Do not allow people who say, "But it was only a dog," put you off. Talk to people who own dogs, preferably other people who have lost an old dog. They understand your grief and your need to talk.

A ceremony can be good too; it is a means for allowing you to say good-bye to your dog and to release some tension. Sprinkling your Aussie's ashes under a fra-grant rose bush or burying it under an apple tree will give you a living monument, a place where you can enjoy nature, where you can recall the wonderful times you shared.

CHAPTER 11

To Breed or Not to Breed

SHOULD YOU BREED? There is really only one reason to breed and that is to produce a litter of dogs that are better than their parents: closer to the breed standard, with fewer faults, and with better working instincts. Even then, your Aussie should not be bred unless homes, responsible homes, are waiting for all of the puppies. Ask yourself the following question: "Am I prepared to keep a litter of puppies for six or more months?" If not, do not breed.

Too many people breed their dog because it "has papers" and they mistakenly believe those registration papers imply quality, which they do not. Registration papers are exactly that, "registration" papers stating the dog's name, date of birth, breed, color, breeder, parents and owner. Just like the registration papers for your car, there is no statement of the dog's quality, or lack of quality, on the papers.

Other dog owners believe a dog is breedable because it comes from champion lines. A pedigree filled with champions is still not enough reason to breed a dog. Other owners, especially those who bought their dog at a pet store for an inflated price, feel they can breed their dog and get their money back because their dog's puppies should sell for as much as it did. Wrong!

Parents often feel their dog should have "just" one litter so their kids can see the miracle of birth. Unfortunately, puppies are rarely born when the kids are around; they arc usually born in the middle of the night. And what happens to those puppies when homes cannot be found for them all? Are the kids going to witness the miracle of death at the Humane Society when those puppies are put to sleep?

Other people love their dog so much they want it to reproduce so they will have another just like it when the old dog passes away. But each puppy is an individual and will never be just like its mother or just like its father. Still others are lead to believe a litter would be snatched up by willing friends and neighbors. But friends may suddenly change their mind about a dog when the prospect of raising a puppy is suddenly thrust upon them.

The dog overpopulation problem is not simply an abundance of mixed breed dogs; it is also a serious problem involving purebreds. In one Southern California city of about 60,000 people, one hundred and fifty dogs a month are destroyed, purebreds and mixed breeds, every month of the year. A similarly sized city in South Carolina had even worse statistics, as did a New York suburb, with over three hundred dog a month destroyed. These three cities, in very different parts of the country, reflect a major problem.

Many purebred dogs are now faced with a variety of debilitating genetic faults and health problems, some of them due to irresponsible breeding. Hip dysplasia, elbow dysplasia, progressive retinal atrophy, collie eye anomaly and other eye defects, skin allergies and a number of other potentially serious faults can be traced to hereditary genes in Australian Shepherds as well as other breeds.

Ch. Brigadoons California Dude CD, HI winning the Stud Dog Class at the USASA National Specialty, 1994, with his get (Ch. Bayshore's Flapjack, Penn Y Caerau's Caught Ya Lookin and Ch. Penn Y Caerau's Northern Lights).

All breeders need to take responsibility for the dogs they produce, taking back dogs that cannot remain in their original homes and admitting when their dogs have produced genetic faults, sharing information with other breeders so that the fault can, hopefully, be eliminated. Too often breeders, embarrassed because their dogs have a fault or defect, hide it from other breeders, and even the new owners of their puppies. Those lines then continue to be used, passing the fault along to more generations, compounding the problem.

Genetics

Genetics is a complicated subject and researchers have spent lifetimes unraveling its mysteries. To simplify it a little, consider that each parent gives its offspring fifty percent of the offspring's genetic material. What results depends upon what that fifty percent is and how it combines with the genetic material from the other parent. The combinations are infinite and are why a brother and sister can be alike or very different.

If you breed a sire to his daughter, a brood bitch to her son, or a brother to a sister, this is called inbreeding. Depending upon how closely related the mother and father were, and whether they were carrying the same recessive genes, the chance of serious defects is increased. Inbreeding is not normally recommended for beginning breeders, but it can be a useful technique for the experienced breeder.

Linebreeding is a form of inbreeding restricted to the pairing of distant relatives.

Linebreeding is used when a breeder wishes to keep the traits of a particularly outstanding dog and so breeds individual dogs to accomplish this. Linebreeding might be a grandmother to a grandson or a grandfather to a granddaughter, for example. When approached wisely, knowing the traits and breeding history of the dogs involved, linebreeding can be more predictable than other breedings in eliminating faults and emphasizing certain positive traits.

Outcrossing is when two unrelated dogs are bred. Although breeders use this when they wish to introduce a different line of dogs, it can be unpredictable as new genetic material is being combined.

A we have seen, the striking merle colors many people admire in the Australian Shepherd are inherited and can have a lethal side. A litter of puppies produced by a merle-to-merle breeding may be deaf or may have eye defects, ranging from minor to complete

Red Merle.

This white-faced bitch exhibits no genetic problems; however, there is a high probability that puppies from a merle to merle breeding who exhibit "pattern white" markings will develope deafness and/or eye disorders.

blindness. The defects associated with merling are not carried by a single gene; they are tied to the recessive genes which produce merle colors and although research is ongoing, it is not thoroughly understood how genes cause the color and how it affects eye and ear development. Therefore, if you have a merle bitch (blue or red) you can breed her to a solid colored dog and therefore reduce the risk of producing defective puppies. If you breed her to another merle, statistically, the odds are one out of four puppies (twenty-five percent) will be a homozygous merle and will have some defect of the eyes or ears. These puppies are usually identified by excessive

white markings surrounding the eyes and on the head and puppies should either be culled at birth or spayed or neutered with registration papers withheld. Although this seems harsh, it is much easier to do at birth than later. Very few deaf or blind dogs can lead any kind of a normal life. They require considerable supervision and restraint and can be difficult to train. However, there is a better chance of avoiding these problems *simply by breeding a merle to a solid color.*

Stud Dog

A stud dog provides fifty percent of the genetic material that will make up the new litter. Although he is half of those new puppies, what is passed to the puppies is not necessarily what you see in the stud dog, but

Breeding your Aussie requires careful thought. In addition to physical appearance, other factors, such as health, genetic background and temperament of of each parent, should be considered.

it is also what he is and what has been passed down to him. For example, he might carry recessive traits you cannot see, but might show up if a brood bitch also carries them.

When selecting an unknown stud dog, it would be wise to do some research and see if you can find some of his littermates. How did they grow up? Do they display any traits you do not like? Keep in mind they share the same genetic material. Look up the sire of your potential stud dog; how do you like him? See if you can find any dogs sired by him with other bitches. Do not be bashful during this process; it is your responsibility as a breeder to produce the best puppies possible.

A stud dog can have a much greater effect on the dog population in general than can the brood bitch because he can,

Wildhagen's Thistle of Flintridge, pictured in April 1970. Thistle is an ASCA Honor Roll Dam and, with Ch. Wildhagen's Dutchman of Flintridge, appears in many pedigrees.

quite simply, be bred to many bitches and hence, pass along his genetic material more often. However, a popular stud dog does not have to be bred to every bitch; in fact, the owner of the stud can and should be selective about who he is bred to, choosing only those bitches that are structurally sound and will complement his type.

Brood Bitch

The brood bitch also provides fifty percent of the genetic material passed on to her puppies, plus her temperament, character and personality all have a great deal of bearing upon the puppies during their first few weeks of life. A nervous, fidgety or shy bitch can pass those traits on to her puppies, both by genetics and by her actions. In addition, her ability to teach and discipline her puppies, from five weeks of age until they go to new homes, can affect how they will relate to other dogs and to their owners throughout their lives.

The brood bitch's health is also vital to the health of her puppies. Her vaccinations should be up to date prior to breeding so she can pass on her immunities to the puppies, and she should be checked for internal parasites and wormed, if necessary. If she has reproductive problems, such as difficulty mating or irregular cycles, or if her mother, grandmother or sister has had reproductive problems, she should not be bred.

Protecting the Standard

Any dog used for breeding should be an excellent specimen, according to the breed standard. The writers of the Australian Shepherd standards did not arbitrarily choose certain characteristics for the Australian Shepherd; rather they selected or stressed attributes that would best serve the breed in its working capacities, keeping the dog as they pictured it should be.

If you have doubts as to how your Aussie measures up to the breed standard, go to a few conformation shows and see how your dog competes against other Australian Shepherds. After the completion of the judging, some judges may be willing to talk to you about your dog. Talk to other people at the show, some may like your dog and others may not, but what is the general consensus?

The standards also say Australian Shepherds are intelligent, attentive and animated, versatile and easily trained. Your Aussie should work with style and enthusiasm and although your dog should be reserved with strangers, it should never show any signs of viciousness towards people or animals. If your Aussie is resistant to training, shows any signs of viciousness, or displays any other traits that would bar it from working, either in obedience or as a stockdog, it should not be bred.

Finally, the breed standards are very clear about the purpose of the Australian Shepherd. The breed is "Primarily a working dog of strong herding and guardian instincts." Although it is unrealistic to demand every breeding Aussie work sheep or cattle on a daily basis, every dog should pass a herding instinct test prior to being added to a breeding program. Any dog that shows no interest in livestock, is uncontrollable or vicious toward the stock should not be used for breeding.

Physical Health

Aussies used for breeding should be physically healthy. This should go without saying, but unfortunately it is not as simple as it might seem. Obvious ailments, such as respiratory disease or parasites, can be identified quite readily, but other problems that can effect the health of the future generations take more investigation.

Eye exams should be done for two years prior to breeding and yearly on breeding dogs, checking for a number of different eye defects, including progressive retinal atrophy (PRA) and collie eye anomaly (CEA). The Canine Eye Registry Foundation, which registers dogs after they have been screened for eye disease, is available for use as a resource by breeders who wish to make sure the stock they are using for breeding is certified clear of eye defects.

Hip dysplasia and elbow dysplasia are crippling diseases in many breeds. In Australian Shepherds, these diseases may cause occasional lameness, soreness during cool weather, arthritis, or permanent disabilities. An affected dog may have one disease, affecting one or both hips or elbows, or it might have both, with all four joints affected. Hip dysplasia is considered by many experts to be a polygenic inherited disorder, which means several factors come into play.

Above, Ch. Blue Isle's Lace Me In Silver at ten weeks, and below right, as an adult.

Many genes may lead to the disease, as well as environmental factors, including exercise and nutrition.

Both the potential sire and dam should be checked for internal and external parasites, and both should be up to date on all vaccinations and be tested for brucellosis, an extremely contagious, incurable canine venereal disease which can cause abortions and other reproductive problems

Mating

A stud dog is capable of siring puppies any time of the year, from about seven months of age until he dies or is too old to physically accomplish the task. However, the American Kennel Club will only accept registrations from sires that are over nine months of age and under twelve years.

A bitch can be bred only when she is in estrus, which for most bitches is every six months, starting any time between six and twelve months of age. Even though a bitch may have hit puberty, she should never be bred before two years of age, for several reasons. First, until that age, the bitch is not mature and it would be cruel to have her bear and raise a litter before she is emotionally and physically ready to do so. Immature bitches often reject their puppies, not understanding what they should do with these strange creatures. Second, the bitch's hips cannot be cleared for hip dysplasia until she is two years old. And last, the bitch's eyes should be checked over a span of two years for eye defects prior to breeding.

As a bitch is coming into the period of reproduction, sometimes called "heat" or "season," maturing eggs will release estrogen, which causes a blood-tinged discharge. At the same time, the vulva (the external genitalia) will swell markedly. The bitch is not ready to

be bred at this time, though she may be flirty and playful, and males will be attracted to the pheromones in her discharge and urine. During this stage, the proestrus, if a male attempts to mount the bitch, she will pull away, sit, or even growl and snap at him.

As the bitch comes into estrus, sometimes called breeding or standing heat, the discharge will clear or become straw colored. The vulva will continue swelling and the bitch's behavior will change. Instead of being flirty, the bitch will turn her back on the male, swinging her hips towards him, arching her back and holding her stub of a tail to the side. When the stud dog mounts her, she will stand to be bred.

FVF Ron D VU Riki of Carolot, Red-tri.

Ch. Bayshore's Flapjack ROM, Best of Breed at the ASCA National Specialty, 1990 and the Westminster Kennel Club show, 1994, is also a multiple Best in Show winner.

When the stud dog mounts the bitch, he will grasp her around the flanks, or waist, with his front legs, holding her tight. The stud dog will thrust several times until he penetrates the vaginal opening. After he has penetrated her, the glandis bulbus will swell, causing the tie. At this time, the stud dog will drop off the bitch, either to her side or turning around and swinging a rear leg over her back. The two usually remain tied for ten to twenty minutes, but ties of up to forty-five minutes are not unusual. When the tie is completed, the glandis bulbus will shrink and he will withdraw his penis.

Although dogs are perfectly capable of reproducing on their own, it is always a good idea to have a couple of people available to help. If the bitch has never been bred before, she may cry out when the stud dog mounts her, or even turn around and bite him. An inexperienced stud dog can be put off if a bitch treats him badly, and many a stud dog sports a torn ear because of a rough encounter. Someone helping the pair can assure that no one is hurt or traumatized unnecessarily. A helper can also make sure the two do not hurt each other while tied; sometimes the bitch will decide to go for a walk, dragging the male behind her.

Ch. Penn Y Caerau's Summer Breeze at eight weeks.

One breeding is usually sufficient for a nice litter, however, many breeders will repeat the breeding two or three times. Do not breed more than once a day or even every day; the stud dog will need a day or two to regenerate a good sperm count. Every other day is fine.

Gestation

Canine gestation is sixty three days although the exact time of whelp may vary from fifty seven to sixty eight days. During the first four weeks of gestation (pregnancy) the bitch should be well fed but not overfed and should be exercised regularly. Stick to her regular routine as much as possible, but protect her from overstrenuous exercise and other dangers that might affect her health and the health of her puppies. For example, be cautious about using insecticides around her; before treating her for fleas, check with your veterinarian.

During the last few weeks of pregnancy, the bitch's appetite will gradually increase. Feed her a good, well-balanced food, preferably one specifically designed for gestating and lactating bitches. She will also need more water, which should always be available. As the puppies grow, they will put pressure on her internal organs and you will want to feed her several smaller meals a day instead of one large meal.

The growing puppies will also put pressure on her bladder and she will need to go outside to relieve herself more often. If she has housetraining accidents, do not make her feel bad; sometimes her bladder may simply "let go."

The week before the puppies are due, the bitch will start to look significantly larger in the belly area, caused by the puppies dropping. Her breasts will start to enlarge and may be pinkish in color.

Several days prior to giving birth, she will start to nest. You may have fixed up a wonderful whelping box, with high sides and comfortable, soft towels as bedding material,

Most bitches nurse their puppies for at least five weeks.

but she may try to choose her own place. If she keeps trying to make a bed in your closet, simply keep bringing her back to her box.

Whelping

The bitch's temperature will drop from the normal of 101.5 degrees F to about 98 degrees prior to the start of labor. Her gums will be pale and she may have a clear mucus discharge from her vulva. She will also start nesting in earnest, scratching at her bedding and circling. She may even try to sneak away to find a spot under the house or out in the garage. Keep a close eye on her or her puppies will be born without your knowledge or help.

During gestation, each puppy is completely enclosed in its own sack, a membrane bag filled with fluid. As the contractions start, each puppy, in its bag, is pushed toward the vagina and birth. The bag may break during delivery or the bitch will tear it away from the puppy's face so it can breath. She will also crush the umbilical cord, and as it is expelled, will eat the placenta. She will then wash the puppy, often very roughly. This stimulation may make the puppies protest loudly, which helps it breathe and gets the pup's circulation going.

Most healthy bitches will be able to whelp normally with little to no assistance from you. However, you need to be present in case there is a problem. Prior to breeding your bitch, you will want to talk to your veterinarian about policies regarding after-hours calls, whelping and so on. He can give you advice about emergencies you might face and what you can do to help. Keep the veterinarian apprised of her due date and have his emergency number by the phone. When her labor starts, call the veterinarian so he can stand by should an emergency occur.

Puppies

The puppies should start to nurse within hours of birth and, needless to say, this is crucial to their well-being. The bitch's first milk will be the colostrum, a concentrated, nourishing milk through which the puppies get their first immunities against disease.

During the first days of life, warmth is a key to survival. Young puppies cannot shiver to stimulate warmth nor can they maintain their own body temperature. An external heat source, such as a heating pad or a heat lamp, can be used to maintain a temperature of 80 to 85 degrees Fahrenheit. Monitor the use of external heat sources because a temperature over 90 degrees Fahrenheit can cause dehydration and death.

Sometime during the first few days you will need to examine each puppy. Occasionally a puppy with an abnormality will survive gestation. It could have been caused by an insecticide or medication that crossed the placental barrier or it could have been caused by a genetic defect. In any case, a puppy with a cleft palate or harelip, or leg or

body deformity should be euthanized. A puppy with excessive white surrounding the eyes or ears should also be euthanized as this is indicative of the recessive genes that cause deafness or eye defects. Luckily, the Australian Shepherd is a healthy breed and deformities are rare except in the case of merle-to-merle breedings, as was explained earlier in this chapter.

You should also identify each puppy. Fortunately, Aussies are among the breeds that produce puppies with enough variation in color and markings that each can be identified by a special mark or color. Even among litters of only blue or red merles, no two puppies will be exactly alike. This process of identification is important because you will be monitoring the growth of each puppy and, in a few short weeks, worming and vaccinating. No puppy should be mistaken for another and overlooked in the process.

Sometime during the first week you will also need to trim the puppies' toenails so they do not scratch the bitch's breasts as they nurse. Using toenails clippers, simply cut off the very tips of the nails, taking care not to trim into the quick. As the puppies grow, trim the nails weekly.

Let the bitch do most of the work taking care of her puppies. She will make sure they relieve themselves by stimulating them as she washes them. She will also keep them close, nosing them closer to her if they wiggle too far away. Be certain she has enough milk; a hungry puppy will be anxious, wiggling and crying. A well-fed pup will sleep when its not eating.

Do not be alarmed when you see the puppies twitching and jerking as they sleep. This "activated sleep" is nature's way of ensuring that newborns get exercise. During a twenty-four hour period, a newborn may move parts of its body hundreds of times.

On the third or fourth day of life, the puppies will need to have its dewclaws removed by your veterinarian. The dewclaw is an extra digit located mid-way on the pastern, similar to the thumb except it is non-functioning. It is usually removed, as it serves no useful purpose and often gets caught on bushes when the dog is working. When a dewclaw catches, it rips the skin or breaks, bleeding and causing the dog severe pain. For conformation show dogs, removing the dew-claw makes the leg look cleaner.

Ch. Las Rocosa Little Wolf, ASCA Hall of Fame Sire.

At the same time, the puppies can have their tails docked, if they need it. Some Aussies are born with a natural bob tail. If the natural tail is four joints or less, you may leave it as is. If the tail is more than four joints, then it should be docked. Most experienced breeders recommend docking the tail between the first and second joint.

The puppies' eyes open when they are ten to thirteen days old. From thirteen to twenty days old, the puppies' nerves and muscles begin to mature and they begin moving more. Temperature control and metabolism are now developing, their ear canals are open and they can hear. At twenty days, some puppies can stand upright and wag their tail—a major accomplishment!

The bitch will start to wean her puppies anytime between the fourth and fifth weeks of life, although you can start some supple-mental feeding anytime during the third and fourth weeks. A flat pie pan works well, as the puppies will not be able to reach over anything higher. A good puppy food recommended by many breeders is as follows: in a blender mix four cups of soaked, high quality puppy food (soaked in a bitch's milk replacement half and half with water), one small can of a high quality dog food (four to five ounce size), a half of a cup baby cereal (rice is good) and enough bitch's replacement milk to make a gruel. Divide the gruel between three or four pie pans, depending upon the number of pup-pies, and supervise the feeding so you know each puppy has eaten something.

By seven weeks the puppies should be weaned and eating on their own. At this

Selling the Puppies

Prior to breeding your bitch, you should have started a list of serious buyers for your litter. Many breeders require a nonrefundable deposit which can be applied to the purchase price. After the birth of the litter, you will then know how many homes are needed, how many buyers you already have and how many more you have to find.

Most breeders use word of mouth to sell their dogs—this is especially true for breeders who have a long standing reputation for breeding quality Aussies. You can call other breeders, put a notice in the breed or training club newsletter, call your friends, put a sign on the bulletin board at work; all of these things can help you sell puppies.

However, simply finding the right number of homes is not your only responsibility; you must also find the right homes. You will be doing both the puppy and the new owner a disservice if you do not help place the right puppy in the most suitable home. For example, if a potential buyer comes to you looking for a puppy for future obedience competition, the shyest most submissive puppy will not be the proper puppy, even if the buyer tries to choose it. A first-time dog owner that is quiet, shy and soft-spoken should not get the biggest, boldest puppy of the litter. It is up to you to help the buyer choose the right puppy. Use the puppy test described in Chapter 2 to help you, as well as the new owner, choose the right puppy.

You do not have to sell a puppy to every person who calls, either. Screen your

time, take them away from the bitch so they do not continue to try to nurse. Start decreasing the gruel and gradually add more puppy food. By the time the puppies are eight to nine weeks of age, they should be eating puppy food only.

At some point prior to the puppies going to their new home you should have them checked for worms or other internal parasites. Collect a stool sample from a puppy or two. Also, weight the lightest and heaviest puppies. With this information your veterinarian will be able to test for worms and prescribe proper doses of medication. Remember, roundworms are common in puppies even if the bitch was wormed prior to mating. The good news is that puppies rarely exhibit any side effects from round worm medication.

callers and if you have doubts, ask for references and then check up on them. When the callers come to see the puppies, watch them. How do they act around your dogs? How do they handle the puppies? How do their children behave? If you are still in doubt, tell them you need to see their yard where the dog will live. Is it safe? Is the fence secure? Is it clean? Would you like to see your puppy living there?

If people call who live in a condo or apartment, tell them you will not sell a puppy to anyone who lives in an apartment: Aussies are not good apartment dogs. Beware the old line, "We're moving next week." Too many times "next week" never comes.

Do not let prospective buyers take a puppy on their first visit. An impulse is the worst reason to get a dog (and, sadly, the one that generates the most pet store puppy sales); instead, let them go home and talk about it and mull it over. If they call back and say they are still interested, this will be a more committed decision.

Use a sales contract for the sale of each puppy. The contract should include your name, address, and telephone as well as the name, address and telephone number of the buyer. It should also identify the puppy, specifying age, breed, sex and markings. The contract should also include any guarantees you offer, such as good health and the absence of hereditary defects (such as hip dysplasia or eye problems). There should also be a place for both your signature and the buyer's signature, as well as the date the contract was signed.

You can also include in the contract a clause stating that you can take back the puppy if you find it has been abused or neglected, has been used for medical research or is being inappropriately used. Under such circumstances, no money should be refunded. (Appendix D is a sample sales contract.)

Put together a package to go with each puppy as it leaves for its new home. Ideally, the package should contain the buyer's copy of the contract, the signed registration papers, a copy of the puppy's pedigree, photographs of the puppy's parents, information about training, herding and other dog activities, and a list of books that might be of interest or help to the new owner. Ahead of time you can make up a list of what constitutes responsible ownership (good food, shelter, exercise, attention, vaccinations, check-ups, licensing, identification and so on) and include this in the puppy package. Include at least two day's worth of the food the puppy has been eating, as well as the name of the food so the new owner can buy the same brand. And last, make sure you give the new owner a list of medications the puppy has had, when its vaccinations were given and if it has been wormed, when and with what medication.

Your responsibility as a breeder does not end when the last puppy goes to its new home. The owners of your puppies should feel free to call you when they have a question or need help. Answer their questions honestly and if you can not help them, refer them to a professional who can. If for some reason the new owners cannot keep their dog, you must be willing to take it back; this can be stipulated in the sales contract.

Watachie's Big Bear of Starcross, CD, CGC, TDI, HC

"Care Bear"

OWNER: LIZ PALIKA
BREEDER: MARIE DAILEY, STARCROSS AUSSIES

During a therapy dog visit to a nursing home, the husband of a recently admitted woman asked us to come to her room for a visit. When I asked the woman if she would like to visit with Care Bear, she replied angrily, "What difference does it make if I visit with a dog? I'm just going to die here."

Care Bear, however, refused to take no for an answer and seemed to know, somehow, that this woman needed his love and affection. Very quietly, he sidled up to her wheelchair and gently stuck his nose under her hand, shoving his head so that her hand ended up on top of his head. Margaret's husband and I pretended to talk, acting like we didn't see what was happening. Within five minutes, Margaret was smiling as she scratched Care Bear's ears. Five visits and a week later, she went home.

Although Care Bear is a wonderful obedience dog, earning several High in Trials, and is accomplished in herding, agility and carting, he shines as a therapy dog. He has a knack for knowing who needs him. His love for the disabled or ill is calm and quiet and surmounts the barriers put up by disease or by differences in cultures or languages.

Spaying or Neutering

Any dog or bitch that does not satisfy the requirements necessary for being used for breeding should be spayed or neutered (castrated). (Actually, neutering applies to either sex, however, general usage has made the word "neuter" apply to castrating a male dog.) Spaying or neutering does not change the dog's personality, nor does it make a dog fat and lazy; however, it does change the dog's metabolism and if the dog's caloric intake is not modified, the dog will gain weight. In bitches, spaying, or ovariohysterectomy, is the removal of the ovaries and uterus. In males, neutering, or castration, consists of removing the testes.

Ch. Brigadoon's Moonraker and his get, ASCA Stud dog class winner, 1982.

Not only does spaying the bitch and neutering the male prevent unwanted pregnancies, but it also reduces the incidence of many cancers later in the dog's life. Spaying a bitch reduces her risk of cancer of the vagina or vulva by over thirty percent. The risk of mammary gland tumors is reduced by two hundred percent or more if she was spayed prior to her first heat. The risk is still reduced by over twelve percent if she was spayed after her first heat. In males, the risk of genital tumors is reduced by over twenty percent after neutering.

Many breeders are now having puppies that do not fit the breed standard spayed or neutered before they are sold to pet or working homes. Previously, most veterinarians recommended dogs be six to seven months of age for neutering. This age was chosen for a number of reasons; at six months, most dogs are physically mature enough that surgery is easier. Also, the risk of putting the dog under anesthesia is better when the puppy is older. Now, with new, safer anesthetics available, the risk of surgery on a puppy is much less. A shelter in Medford, Oregon has been neutering puppies at a young age for more than ten years with no reports of ill affects.

A well-documented benefit of spaying and neutering, especially early-age surgery, is the more passive temperament of the dog. With the drive to reproduce eliminated, Aussie can focus on you and on training, either for stock work, obedience or any other dog sport. It will live longer, with a reduced risk of cancer, and will not be driven by hormones to reproduce.

As a side benefit, by spaying or neutering your Aussie, you will save money. Breeding is not cheap, with stud dog fees, extra nutrition for the bitch during gestation and lactation, veterinarian's fees, the whelping box, supplemental feedings for the puppies, advertising, feeding the puppies, copying the pedigrees and applying for the litter registration.

Australian Shepherd Rescue

Unfortunately, sometimes an Aussie is not able to live out its life in the original home. There could be many reasons for this, resulting in a situation where a good dog needs to find a new, loving family. Often Australian Shepherd Rescue can help. Aussie Rescue and Placement Helpline (ARPH) is organized by members of the Australian Shepherd Club of America. Their goal is to screen rescued Australian Shepherds and potential adoptive homes so the right dog can be adopted by the right family. Local clubs and groups also do rescue work, saving deserving dogs that might otherwise be destroyed. If you would like more information about ARPH call 1-800-892-ASCA.

Appendix A
Organizations & For More Information

American Dog Packing Association
2154 Woodlyn Road
Pasadena, CA 91104

American Herding Breed Association
1548 Victoria Way
Pacifica, CA 94044

American Kennel Club
51 Madison Avenue
New York, NY 10010

American Temperment Test Society
P.O. Box 397
Fenton, MO 63026

Australian Shepherd Club of America
Business Office
6091 East State Highway 21
Bryan, TX 77803-9652

Canine Eye Registration Foundation (CERF)
Veterinary Medical Data Program
South Campus Courts, Building C
Purdue University, West Lafayette, IN 47907
317-494-8179

Dog Fancy Magazine
(article reprints/back issues)
P.O. Box 6050
Mission Viejo, CA 92690

Dog World Magazine
(article reprints/back issues)
29 North Wacker Drive
Chicago, IL 60606

Friskies Canine Frisbee Disc Championships
4060 D Peachtree Road, Suite 326G
Atlanta, GA 30319
800-786-9240

International Council for Sleddog Sports
Route 1, Box 670
Grand Marais, MN 5604
218-387-2712

International Federation of Sled Dog Sports
1763 Indian Valley Road
Novato, CA 94947

International Weight Pulling Association
P.O. Box 994
Greeley, CO 80632

Landesverband DVG America (Schutzhund)
113 Vickie Drive
Del City, OK 73115

National Association for Search and Rescue
P.O. Box 3709
Fairfax, VA 22309

National Dog Registry
(tattoo registry/lost and found)
P.O. Box 116
Woodstock, NY 12498

North American Dog Agility Council
(NADAC)
HCR 2, Box 277
St. Maries, ID 83861

North American Flyball Association
1 Gooch Park Drive
Barrie, Ontario, Canada L4M 4S6

Orthepedic Foundation for Animals (OFA)
University of Missouri
Columbia, MO 65211
314-442-0418

Progressive Retinal Atrophy Research (PRA)
P.O. Box 15095
San Francisco, CA 94115

Therapy Dogs International
6 Hilltop Rd.
Mendham, NJ 07945

Trans-National Dog Agility
410 Bluemont Circle
Manhattan, KS 66502

United Kennel Club
100 East Kilgore Road
Kalamazoo, MI 49001-5598
616-343-9020

United Schutzhund Clubs of America
3704 Lemoy Ferry Road
St Louis, MO 63125

U.S. Dog Agility Association
P.O. Box 850955
Richardson, TX 75085-0955

Ch. Coppertones Cactus of Bonnie Blu.

Appendix B
Sample Entry Form

1. Name of the club hosting the show.
Date of the show.
Location of the show.
How much the entry fee is.
Where to send it.
The closing or due date of the entry.

2. Breed of dog.

3. Male or Female.

4. Conformation (breed competition) show class: Puppy, Open, Bred-by-Exhibitor, etc.

5. Color variety: Blue Merle, Red Merle, Black, etc.

6. If entered in more than one class, enter the second class here.

7. Obedience trial class entered: Novice A, Open, etc.

8. The name and identification number of Junior Handler if he/she is competing in the Junior Handling competition (also see the back of an entry form for further details needed for this competition).

9. Dog's registered name.

10. Dog's registration number from the sponsoring organization (AKC, ASCA or other).

11. Dog's date of birth.

12. Dog's place of birth.

13. Name of Breeder(s).

14. Sire (dog's father).

15. Dam (dog's mother).

16. Name of owner(s) as it appears on the registration.

17. Owner's address, or where you want the entry confirmation sent.

18. Name of the individual showing the dog if the owner is not.

19. Signature of the owner or owner's agent (the person showing the dog).

OFFICIAL CLUB ENTRY FORM

1

PLEASE TYPE OR PRINT IN BLACK INK ONLY

I ENCLOSE $ for entry fees

IMPORTANT--Read Carefully Instructions on Reverse Side Before Filling Out Numbers in the boxes indicate sections of the instructions revelant to the information needed in that box (PLEASE PRINT)

BREED 2	VARIETY [1]	SEX 3

DOG [2] [3] SHOW CLASS 4	CLASS [3] DIVISION 5 Weight color etc

ADDITIONAL CLASSES 6	OBEDIENCE TRIAL CLASS 7	JR SHOWMANSHIP CLASS

NAME OF (See Back) JUNIOR HANDLER (if any) 8

FULL NAME OF DOG 9

□ AKC REG NO □ AKC LITTER NO □ I L P NO □ FOREIGN REG NO & COUNTRY Enter number here 10	DATE OF BIRTH 11
	PLACE OF BIRTH □ U S A □ Canada □ Foreign 12 Do not print the above in catalog

BREEDER 13

SIRE 14

DAM 15

ACTUAL OWNER(S) 16   (Please Print)
[4]
OWNER'S ADDRESS 17

CITY _____ STATE _____ ZIP _____

NAME OF OWNER'S AGENT (IF ANY) AT THE SHOW 18

I CERTIFY that I am the actual owner of the dog, or that I am the duly authorized agent of the actual owner whose name I have entered above In consideration of the acceptance of this entry I (we) agree to abide by the rules and regulations of The American Kennel Club in effect at the time of this show or obedience trial, and by any additional rules and regulations appearing in the premium list for this show or obedience trial or both, and further agree to be bound by the "Agreement" printed on the reverse side of this entry form I (we) certify and represent that the dog entered is not a hazard to persons or other dogs This entry is submitted for acceptance on the foregoing representation and agreement

SIGNATURE of owner or his agent duly authorized to make this entry 19

TELEPHONE # _____

Ch. Shady Acres Irish Lyric.

Ch. Moonlights Hotest Thing Goin', Best of Breed at the ASCA National Specialty, 1993.

Appendix C
Conformation Competition

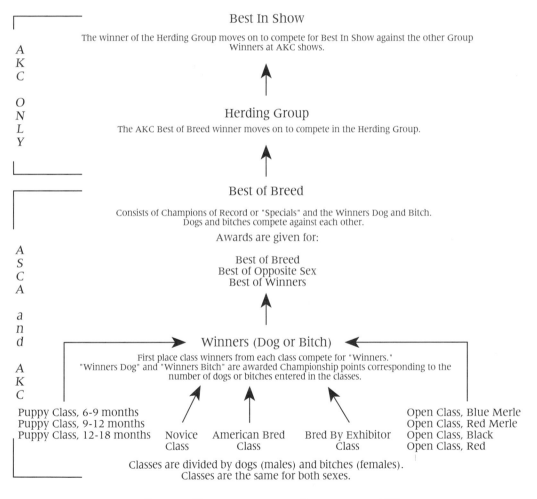

Best In Show

The winner of the Herding Group moves on to compete for Best In Show against the other Group Winners at AKC shows.

↑

Herding Group

The AKC Best of Breed winner moves on to compete in the Herding Group.

↑

Best of Breed

Consists of Champions of Record or "Specials" and the Winners Dog and Bitch.
Dogs and bitches compete against each other.

Awards are given for:

Best of Breed
Best of Opposite Sex
Best of Winners

↑

Winners (Dog or Bitch)

First place class winners from each class compete for "Winners."
"Winners Dog" and "Winners Bitch" are awarded Championship points corresponding to the number of dogs or bitches entered in the classes.

A
K
C

O
N
L
Y

A
S
C
A

a
n
d

A
K
C

Puppy Class, 6-9 months
Puppy Class, 9-12 months
Puppy Class, 12-18 months

Novice
Class

American Bred
Class

Bred By Exhibitor
Class

Open Class, Blue Merle
Open Class, Red Merle
Open Class, Black
Open Class, Red

Classes are divided by dogs (males) and bitches (females).
Classes are the same for both sexes.

Conformation or "Breed" Competition

Appendix D
Sample Puppy Sales Contract

I, _____ the breeder/owner of the said puppy (described below), hereafter "Seller," do enter into an agreement with _____, hereafter "Buyer" for the purpose of transferring ownership of the said puppy.

The said puppy is a purebred Australian Shepherd, male/female, sired by
_____, out of _____. The puppy is _____
(color) with _____
_____ markings. The said puppy's date of birth is
_____ and registration papers with AKC/ASCA or other registries _____
are/are not included as part of this agreement. The registration papers will include, as part of the puppy's name, the _____ kennel name.

The Seller will transfer ownership of the said puppy for $_____, to be paid in full.

The Seller guarrantees that the said puppy is in good health at the time of this agreement. The Buyer agrees to have the puppy examined by a veterinarian within 48 hours of this agreement. If the puppy is determined to be in poor health, the Buyer can elect to keep the puppy, assuming all costs for its care, or may return the puppy for a full refund upon the Seller's receipt of the veterinarian's statement regarding the puppy's health.

The Seller warrants that the puppy is the progeny of breeding dogs examined and cleared of eye defects, and x-rayed and cleared for hip and elbow dysplasia. If the puppy develops eye defects, or hip or elbow dysplasia within twelve months from the date of birth, the Buyer may return the dog to the Seller for either a replacement dog from the next litter, or may keep the said puppy, which then must be spayed or neutered. If the Buyer keeps the said puppy, the Seller will refund $_____ upon verification of eye defects or dysplasia.

The Buyer agrees that the puppy will not be used for breeding until at least two years of age and only after the puppy has been examined at least twice for eye defects and has been cleared; and only after the puppy has been x-rayed and cleared of both hip and elbow dysplasia. If the puppy is determined to have eye defects, dysplasia, communicable diseases and/or hereditary defects or faults, it shall not be used for breeding and shall be spayed or neutered.

If the Seller determines (prior to this agreement) that the puppy is pet quality, the registration papers will be withheld until the Buyer provides certification from a veterinarian that the puppy has been spayed or neutered.

If, at some time in the future, the Buyer is unable to keep the puppy, he/she will contact the Seller before taking any action, so that the Seller can buy back the puppy, if he/she so desires.

The Buyer certifies, by signing this contract, that the puppy will live with the Buyer, be confined by a fenced yard, will have adequate exercise, nutritious food, and necessary health care, including yearly vaccinations.

Upon completion of an obedience training class and receipt of a copy of the certificate, the Seller will refund to the Buyer the amount of $_____.

Upon completion of a conformation championship, obedience titles, stockdog titles or other performance events, the Seller will refund or award $_____.

The Buyer certifies, by signing this contract, that he/she is not acting as an agent in this purchase; that the Buyer will not resell this puppy to a pet store, guard dog business or medical research facility.

This contract is made and signed by both the Seller and the Buyer for the well-being of the said puppy. If any part of this contract is breached by the Buyer, the Seller can and will reposess the puppy.

Seller's Signature_____Date _____
Seller's Printed Name _____
Seller's Kennel Name _____
Seller's Address_____
City_____State____ Zip_____
Seller's Telephone (day)_____(eves)_____

Buyer's Signature_____Date_____
Buyer's Printed Name _____
Buyer's Address_____
City_____State____Zip_____
Buyer's Telephone (day)_____(eves)_____

Appendix E
Available Titles

Australian Shepherd Club of America

CONFORMATION
>Champion - Ch.

OBEDIENCE
>Companion Dog - CD
>Companion Dog Excellent - CDX
>Utility Dog - UD
>Tracking Dog - TD
>Tracking Dog Excellent - TDX
>Obedience Trial Champion - OTCH

STOCKDOG
>Started Trial Dog - STD
>Open Trial Dog - OTD
>Advanced Trial Dog - ATD
>Working Trial Champion - WTCH
>Ranch Dog - RD
>Ranch Trial Dog - RTD

COMBINATION
>Versatility Champion - VCH
>Supreme Versatility Champion-SVCH

American Kennel Club

CONFORMATION
>Champion - Ch.

OBEDIENCE
>Companion Dog - CD
>Companion Dog Excellent - CDX
>Utility Dog - UD
>Utility Dog Excellent - UDX
>Obedience Trial Champion - OTCH

TRACKING
>Tracking Dog - TD
>Tracking Dog Excellent - TDX

HERDING
>Herding Tested - HT
>Pre-trial Tested - PT
>Herding Started - HS
>Herding Intermidiate - HI
>Herding Advanced - HX
>Herding Trial Champion - HCh.

AGILITY
>Novice Agility Dog - NAD
>Open Agility Dog - OAD
>Agility Dog Excellent - ADX
>Master Agility Excellent - MAX

*WTCH Windsong's Shenanigan CD and WTCH Twin
Oaks Windsong CDX, ASCA Hall of Fame dams.*

WTCH Ch. Windsong's Raisin' Cain, ASCA Hall of Fame Sire.

Appendix F
The Australian Shepherd Club of America Hall of Fame
Courtesy of The Australian Shepherd Club of America

Requirements

Kennels - Must have produced ten dual-titled dogs, with a minimum of a conformation Championship and one of the following: CDX, OTD (cattle or sheep) or ATD (ducks).

Sires - Must have produced eight champion get or eight CDX titles or eight OTD (cattle or sheep) or eight ATD (ducks) or any combination of these titles, totaling eight.

Dams - Must have produced twelve champion titles or twelve CDX titles or twelve OTD (cattle or sheep) or eight ATD (ducks) or any combination of these titles, totaling twelve.

Versatility - Dog or Bitch must have Ch., CDX, two OTD and one ATD; a CD and TD may be substituted for the CDX.

Supreme Versatility - Dog or Bitch must have Ch., UD and WTCH.

	Kennels	Owners
001	Las Rocosa	The Hartnagle Family
002	Propwash Farm	Leslie B. Frank
003	Slash V Ranch	Terry Martin
004	Diamond Aire	Marie Murphy
005	Windermere	Stewart & Judy Williams
006	Twin Oaks	Klarer, Hayes, Baker, Sisson
007	Starcross	Marie Dailey
008	Beauwood	Debra St. Jacques
009	Casa Buena	Neil & Jeanne Weaver
010	Heatherhill	Alan & Kathy McCorkle

Sires

	Dog	**Owner**
001	Ch. Briarbrook's Center Ring	Lorna Luce
002	Ch. Fieldmaster of Flintridge	Marcia Hall
003	Ch. Fieldmaster's Three Ring Circus	Linda Wilson
004	Ch. Fieldmaster's Blue Isle Barnstormer	Linda Wilson
005	Ch. Briarbrook's Checkmate	Linda Wilson
006	Ch. Las Rocosa Shiloh	Elaine & Jeanne Joy Hartnagle
007	Las Rocosa Sydney	Elaine Hartnagle
008	Las Rocosa Lester	Leo Foure
009	Ch. Hemi's Regal Request, CD, STDs, OTDd	Gary & Mary Hawley
010	Ch. Hallmark of Windemere, OTDd	Gary & Mary Hawley
011	WTCH Ch. Windsong's Raisin Cain, CD	Rick Dill
012	Ch. Brigadoon's One Arrogant Dude	Bonnie Daniel
013	Ch. Arrogance of Heatherhill, CD, STDd	Kathy McCorkle & Bonnie Daniel
014	Ch. Bayshore's Three to Get Ready, CD, STDd	Frank Baylis & Marge Stovall
015	Ch. Jimmee Blue of Adelaide, CD	Pam Bethurum
016	Ch. Chulo Rojo of Fairoaks	Sandy Cromwell
017	Ch. Briarbrook's Game Plan	Terri Morgan & Selena Poplin
018	Ch. Windermere's Sunshine of Bonnie-Blu, CDX	Stewart & Judy Williams
019	WTCH Ch. Beauwood's Rustlin' In the Sun, CDX, TD, RDX	Debra & Mark St. Jacques
020	Ch. Las Rocosa Little Wolf STDcd	Jeanne Hartnagle-Taylor
021	Ch. Jubilee's Federal Agent	Barbara Peters
022	Ch. Some Like It Hot of Adelaide	Tina Burks
023	WTCH Ch. Apache Tears of Timberline, UDT	Nick Davi
024	WTCH Little Spot's Speckled Image	Pat Lambeth
025	Ch. Peachcreek's Razzle Dancer	Rob & Nan Gilliard
026	Ch. Aristocrat's Once Ina Blue Moon	Janeen Hudson & Linda Wilson
027	Ch. Beauwood's Out Rustlin' Bear, UDT, OTDd, STDcs	Debra St. Jacques
028	WTCH Zephyr's Crimson King, RDX	Tony Rohne
029	Ch. Copper Canyon Caligari, CD	Lois George
030	George's Red Rustler	Lois George
031	WTCH Windsong's Hurrah Cain, CD	Chris Timmons
032	WTCH The Bear of Twin Oaks	Boyce & Sherry Baker
033	Ch. Yankee Clipper of Wingmont	Brenda & Don Dean
034	Ch. Rosewoods Red Hot Special	Richard Pittman
035	Ch. Brookridge's Quincys Invasion, CD	Susan Moorehead

036	Ch. Tri-Ivory Roquefort of Higgins, CD	Richard, Charlene, Shaul & Sheila Polk
037	Ch. Briarbrook's Bishop of Wynridge, CD STDdsc	Terri Morgan & Selena Poplin
038	WTCH The Bull of Twin Oaks, CD, RDX, RTDs	Cee Hambo
039	WTCH Las Rocosa Kublia Kahn Crown Pt., RDX	Wayne & Kaye Harris
040	Ch. Coppertone's East of the Sun, CD	Pepper Ludwig Schroeder
041	Ch. Fantasia's Master Peace	Anna & David Gibbons
042	Ch. Winchester's Hotline	Judy Chard
043	Ch. Showtime's Sir Prize, CD	Flo McDaniel & Susan L. Rossy
044	WTCH Las Rocosa Bonny Kyle, RDX	Kerry Russell

Dams

	BITCH	**OWNERS**
001	Slash V Semi Sweet, OTDcd, STDs	Terry Martin
002	Ch. Ebony Eyes of Fireside	Marie Dailey
003	Encore's SeMeGo for Quatro K, UD, STDc	Preston & Annette Kissman
004	Aristocrat's lady Sings the Blues	Linda Wilson
005	Ch. Patch-Work Quilt	Linda Wilson
006	Twin Oaks Poky Cody, OTDcd, STDs	Audrey Klarer
007	Ch. Fancy Fan Fair of Las Rocosa, STDc	Ernest Hartnagle
008	Ch. Snow's Regal Cactus Berry, CD	Hazel & Rondal Snow
009	Aristocrat's My Lady of Fairview	Maria Pino
010	Ch. Pepper Tree's Free Dawn	Leslie B. Frank
011	Ch. Sitting Pretty of Sunnybrook	Frank Baylis
012	Ch. Bayshore's Mi La May	Frank Baylis
013	WTCH Parrish's Illusion, CD	Marti Parrish
014	Ch. Diamond Airebell, CD, STDd	Marie Murphy
015	Ch. Vanlandingham's Ebony Lace, CD, OTDd	Laurel Vanlandingham
016	Ch. Briarbrook's Song and Dance, CD	Rob & Nan Gilliard
017	Briarbrook's Marque of Patchwork	Linda Wilson
018	Ch. Starswept's Sky's the Limit	Carol Earnest
019	Ch. Popwash Positively, CD	Leslie B. Frank
020	Fisher's Blue Heather of Windermere	Stewart & Judy Williams
021	WTCH Windsong's Shenanigan, CD	Kathy Warren
022	WTCH Twin Oak's Windsong, CDX	Kathy Warren
023	WTCH Windsong's City Rhythm	Melinda Warren
024	Ch. Twin Oaks Spinner, STDd	Sherry Baker
025	Las Rocosa Poco Lena, ATDsd, OTDc	Neil & Jeanne Weaver

026	Ch. Bumblebee's Sassy First Love, CD, OTDd	Vianne Paula Carlson
027	Ch. Briarbrook's Sheer Emotions, CD	Susan Moorehead
028	Ch. Slash V Slide Me Sweet, CD	Red Oliver
029	Ch. Brushwood Bonnie Kye, CD, OTDcs, ATDd	Canby & Sherrie Scott
030	Ch. Country Hotline of Agua Dulce, CDX	Tiffany D. Levin
031	Ch.Windsong's Foggi Notion	Dan & Sherry Ball
032	Ch.Blue Moon on Stillwaters, CDX, TD, STDds	Kristine Martinson
034	Ch. Moonshine of Windermere	Brenda Dean & Leslie B. Frank
035	WTCH Oliver's Jamie RDg	John Hart
036	Kindle's Rusty Rose	Raymond C. Kindle
037	Ch. Briarbrook's Frosty Mint	Anna & David Gibbons
038	Ch. Marqui Sun-Up Sarah McMatt	Matt & Flo McDaniel

Versatility

	Dog	**Owner**
001	Casa Buena Kameo, CDX, OTDc, ATDsd	Lori Middleton
002	WTCH Ch. Talkooks Yahoo Charlie, CDX, RDg	Marten Walter
003	Ch. Shanti's Rowdy Rustler, CDX OTDc, ATDsd	Ken Lyle
004	WTCH Ch. Gitalong's Half Cocked, CDX	Kristine & Paul Martinson
005	WTCH Ch. Gold Nugget's Cock of the Walk, CD, TD	Danny & Judy Norris
006	Ch. Spring Fever Mollie Rock, CDX, OTDcs, ATDd	Robyn Nelson
007	Ch. Spring Fever's Jutterbug, CDX, OTDcs, ATDd	Robyn Nelson

Supreme Versatility

| 001 | WTCH Ch. Apache Tears of Timberline, UDT | Nick Davis |

George's Red Rustler, ASCA Hall of Fame Sire.

Ch. Windermere's Sunshine of Bonnie-Blu CD, ASCA Hall of Fame Sire and Best of Breed at the ASCA National Specialty 1976.

Appendix G
Australian Shepherd Club of America National Specialty Winners
Courtesy of The Australian Shepherd Club of America

APRIL 6, 1974,

68 Dogs   76 Bitches

BOB: Ch. Farrington's Buster Ivory, ASUD
BOS: Ch. Fromers Free Breeze, CD
WD: Quinlowe's Homre
BOW & WB: Tri-Ivory Anna Banana

NOVEMBER 29, 1975

78 Dogs   77 Bitches

BOB: Ch. Pay the Piper of Aberdare, CD
BOS: CH. Posey Patch of Blue Mist
BOW & WD: Tri-Ivory Yankee Dandy
WB: Sweet Season of Heatherhill
High in Working Trial: Rowe's Commanche Warrior

SEPTEMBER 4, 1976

75 Dogs   82 Bitches

BOB: Ch. Windermere's Sunshine of Bonnie-Blu, CDX
BOS: Ch. Summer Breeze of Sunnybrook
BOW & WD: Copper Canyon's Caligari
WB: Winter Wishes of Windermere
High in Working Trial: Mini Acre Peppermint Patti

SEPTEMBER 3, 1977

95 Dogs   69 Bitches

BOB: Copper Canyon Caligari
BOS: Ch. Maranatha Velvet Morning of Heatherhill
BOW & WD: Copper Canyon Caligari
WB: Sadie J. of Coppertone
High in Obedience Trial: Granzow's Rowdie Girl
High in Working Trial: Willadee's Freckle Face

SEPTEMBER 2, 1978
59 Dogs   73 Bitches
BOB: Ch. Wee Willie of Windermere
BOS: Ch. Patch-Work Pollyana, CD
BOW & WD: Sundowner's Boomerang, CD
WB: Windsong's Foggi Notion

SEPTEMBER 1, 1979
77 Dogs   101 Bitches
BOB: Ch. Somercrest Copper Wiggles of Talkook
BOS: Ch. Tri-Ivory Ruff Rider, CD
BOW & WD: Tri-Ivory Crusader Rabbit
WB: Sweet Dreams of Stardust
High in Obedience Trial: Ch. Starshine of Windermere
High in Worling Trial: Bruton's Holtex
High in Working Trial: Ch. Power River's City Slicker
Most Versatile: Ch. Blue Lad Black Velvet, CD

AUGUST 30, 1980
66 Dogs   81 Bitches
BOB: Ch. Tri-Ivory Yankee Dandy, CDX, RDc
BOS: Ch. Somercrest Copper Wiggles of Talkook
BOW & WD: Fieldmaster's Pizza De Action
WB: Nelson's Phoebe of Gold Nugget
High in Obedience Trial: Tri-Ivory Baked Alaska
High in Working Trial: Smithfields Calico Lady
High in Working Trial: Sage's Kelly Blue, CDX
Most Versatile: Ch. Apache Tears of Timberline, UD, OTD, ATD

OCTOBER 10, 1981
128 Dogs   163 Bitches
BOB: Ch. Tri-Ivory Yankee Dandy, CDX, RDc
BOS: Ch. Echo Pines Blue Feather Maid
BOW & WD: Tri-Ivory Sam of Ridgetop
WB: Windhill's Miss Muffet
High in Obedience Trial: Ch. Beauwood's Out Rustlin' Bear, CDX, STDd
High in Working Trial: Windsong's Troya, STDd, OTDs, ATDc
Most Versatile: Donegal's Travelin' Man, STDdsc

SEPTEMBER 4, 1982
86 Dogs   98 Bitches
BOB: Aristocrat's Once In A Blue Moon
BOS: Ch. All That Jazz of Gefion, CD, STD
BOW & WD: Aristocrat's Once In A Blue Moon
WB: Shadow fax Black Gold
High in Obedience Trial: Sugar Bear's Tobe, CD
High in Working Trial: Casa de Carrillo Callie
High in Working Trial: Black Powder's Kizzy Stub, CD, ATDc, STDsd
Most Versatile: Ch. Apache Tears of Timberline, UD, OTDc, ATDsd

SEPTEMBER 16, 1983
79 Dogs   85 Bitches
BOB: Ch. Fieldmaster's Blue Isle Barnstormer
BOS: Ch. All That Jazz of Gefion
BOW & WD: Tri-Ivory Just Dandy
WB: Briarbrook's Kizzy of Natahni
High in Obedience Trial: Tri-Ivory Just Dandy
High in Working Trial: Los Rocosa Merlin Hart, RD, STDdc, ATDd
Most Versatile: WTCH Ch. Apache Tears of Timberline, UDT

OCTOBER 12, 1984
121 Dogs   156 Bitches
BOB: Ch. Windhill's Blue Spectre, CD
BOS: Ch.   Visions of Firside
BOW & WD: Scotch Em Brandy
WB: Scalawag's Annie's Song
High in Obedience Trial: Ken-Lins Black Lace Nightie
High in Working Trial: WTCH Windsong's City Rhythm
Most Versatile: Touch O'Silver Goat Roper, CDX

SEPTEMBER 20, 1985

113 Dogs   172 Bitches

BOB:	Ch. Tri-Ivory Roquefort of Higgins, CD
BOS:	Ch. Riveara of Brigadoon
BOW & WD:	Brigadoon's California Dude
WB:	Twin Oaks Taste of Burgandy, CDX
High in Obedience Trial:	Black Point's Shadow Rustler
High in Working Trial:	Justus N Molly McGee, STDcsd
High in Working Trial:	Mighty Fine Second Chance
Most Versatile:	Lawson's Cool Shamus, UD, OTDs, ATDd

OCTOBER 9, 1986

78 Dogs   127 Bitches

BOB:	Ch. Steal the Show of Bainbridge
BOS:	Ch. Gold Nugget's Blue Cheese
WD:	Peachcreeks Razzle Dancer
BOW & WB:	Propwash Poplolly, CD
High in Obedience Trial:	All That Glamour of Sunwood
High in Working Trial:	Slash V Slide Me Sweet, ATDs, OTDcd
High in Working Trial:	Ch. Cas Buena Kameo, CDX, OTDc, ATDds
Most Versatile:	Ch. Gold Nugget's Blue Cheese

NOVEMBER 25, 1987

155 Dogs   233 Bitches

BOB:	Ch. Some Like It Hot of Adelaide
BOS: Intl./ASCA/Mex.	Ch. Dynamite Dazzle of Starcross, CDX
BOW & WD:	Agua Dulce Final Option
WB:	Peachcreeks Handulla Charm
High in Obedience Trial:	Ch. Wyldewood's Chorus Line
High in Working Trial:	WTCH Hangin' Tree's Red Zephyr, RDX
Most Versatile:	Iron Eyes Kody of Woodstock, STDs

NOVEMBER 2, 1988

157 Dogs   240 Bitches

BOB:	Ch. Tri-Ivory Roquefort of Higgins, CD
BOS:	Peachcreeks Song of the South
WD:	Showtimes Just Ah-Some
BOW & WB:	Peachcreeks Song of the South
High in Obedience Trial:	JKS Brown Einstein
High in Working Trial:	Crown Pt. Inspirator Bar LW
Most Versatile:	Ch. Beauwood's Rustlin' In The Sun

Stockdog Finals

    Champion Duck, Sheep, Cattle Dog: WTCH Slash V Slide Me Sweet, CD

OCTOBER 4, 1989

135 Dogs   206 Bitches

BOB:	Ch. Gingerbreads Oh So Arrogant
BOS:	Ch. Lady in Red of Heatherhill
BOW & WD:	Stardust's Just Incredible
WB:	Jubilee's Magic Slipper
High in Obedience Trial:	Vaquero's Rowdy O Shep, CDX
High in Working Trial:	WTCH The Bull of Twin Oaks, RDX
Most Versatile:	Oxford's Countess of Caligari

Stockdog Finals

    Champion Duck Dog: WTCH Windsong's City Rhythm

    Champion Sheep Dog: WTCH Twin Oaks Kit Carson

    Champion Cattle Dog: WTCH The Bull of Twin Oaks, RDX

SEPTEMBER 26, 1990

204 Dogs   291 Bitches

BOB:	Ch. Bayshore's Flapjack
BOS:	Ch. Peachcreek's Song of the South
BOW & WD:	Peachcreek's Above the Law
WB:	Tri-Ivory Caress
High in Obedience Trial:	Ch. Shady Acre Run Four the Roses
High in Working Trial:	WTCH Twin Oaks Kit Carson, RDX
Most Versatile:	VCH WTCH Ch. Gitalong's Half Cocked, CDX

Stockdog Finals

    Champion Duck, Sheep Dog: WTCH Twin Oaks Kit Carson

    Champion Cattle Dog: WTCH Slash V Slide Me Sweet, CD

OCTOBER 8, 1991

126 Dogs   163 Bitches

BOB:	Ch. Briarbrook's State of the Art, CD
BOS:	Ch. Oprah Winfree of Heatherhill
BOW & WD:	Meri-Mers Top Gun of Chrisdava
WB:	Propwash Manape' Cracklin' Rosie
High in Obedience Trial:	Kanyaka The Wonder Dog
High in Working Trial:	WTCH The Bull of Twin Oaks, CD, RDX
Most Versatile:	VCH WTCH Ch. Gitalong's Half Cocked, CDX

Stockdog Finals

Champion Duck, Sheep, Cattle Dog: WTCH The Bull of Twin Oaks, CD, RDX

NOVEMBER 17, 1992

221 Dogs   312 Bitches

BOB:	Ch. Propwash Flounce
BOS:	Ch. My Main Man of Heatherhill
WD:	Rich and Famous of Heatherhill
BOW & WB:	Bay View's Soda of Gold Nugget
High in Obedience Trial:	Gold Nugget's Cisco Kid, CD
High in Working Trial:	WTCH Twin Oaks Kit Carson, RDX
Most Versatile:	Ch. Southern Cross Crimson King, CD, STDsd

Stockdog Finals

Champion Duck, Cattle Dog: WTCH Twin Oaks Kit Carson, RDX

Champion Sheep Dog: WTCH Windsong's Flintrip

OCTOBER 13, 1993

113 Dogs   172 Bitches

BOB:	Ch. Moonlights Hottest Thing Goin
BOS:	Ch. Donegal's Four Seasons
BOW & WD:	Gitalong's Ooooz N Ahhz
WB:	Nightwind Dancin with Topgun
High in Obedience Trial:	Gitalong's Boogie Woogie
High in Working Trial:	WTCH Twin Oaks Kit Carson, RDX
Most Versatile:	Ch. Indian Run Snoqualmie, CD, STDds, OTDc

Stockdog Finals

Champion Duck Dog: WTCH O'Sage's Shinen Times

Champion Sheep, Cattle Dog: WTCH Twin Oaks Kit Carson, RDX

Ch. Las Rocosa Leslie CD, ASCA Honor Roll Dam.

Ch. Tri-Ivory Yankee Dandy, Winners Dog and Best of Winners at the ASCA National Specialty, 1975 and Best of Breed at the ASCA National Specialty, 1980 and 1981.

Photo Credits

4, 24, 26, 27, 28, 29, 30, 32, 33, 39, 40, 42, 44, 45, 46 (Left), 48, 49, 51, 52, 53, 57, 68, 77, 78, 80, 86, 87, 88, 96 (Right), 104 (Left), 110, 111 (Bottom), 112, 113, 114, 115, 116, 117 (Top), 118, 119 (Bottom), 120, 128 (Top), 129 (Bottom Right), 130, 131, 132, 133, 134, 136, 137, 141, 142, 143, 144, 152, 153, 154, 155, 156, 163, 167, 170, 174, 177, 178, 182 (Top), 184, 187, 196, 215, 221: *Steve Eltinge*

6: *Evelyn Cameron, Courtesy of The Montana Historical Society, Helena*

8: *Unknown, Courtesy of The Wyoming State Museum*

9: *Unknown, Courtesy of The Wyoming State Museum*

10: *Unknown, Courtesy of The State Agricultural Heritage Museum, South Dakota State University*

11: *Unknown, Courtesy of The Wyoming State Museum*

12: *The Solomon D. Butcher Collection, Courtesy Nebraska State Historical Society*

13 (Left), 79, 113 (Bottom): *Unknown, Courtesy of Vicky Mistretta*

13 (Right), 94, 95: *Unknown, Courtesy of Don Lawson*

14, 16 (Left): *Larry Landsberg*

15: *Floyd H. McCall, Courtesy of Mr. and Mrs. Jay Sisler*

16 (Right): *Jay Sisler*

17 (Left & Right), 19 (Bottom), 186, 213 (Top): *Jeanne Joy Hartnagle-Taylor, Las Rocosa Aussie's*

18 (Left): *Dr. Weldon Heard, Courtesy of J. Frank Baylis, Bayshore Farms*

18 (Right), 50: *Terry Martin*

19 (Top): *Dr. Weldon Heard*

20 (Left), 99: *Unknown, Courtesy of Phil Wildhagen*

21 (Left), 46 (Right), 47: *Leslie Frank*

21 (Right), 103 (Left): *Chuck and Sandy Tatham, Courtesy of Leslie Frank, Propwash Farm*

22: *Ashbey Photo, Courtesy of J. Frank Baylis, Bayshore Farms*

23: *Unknown, Courtesy of Gary and Mary Hawley*

34, 35, 36, 37, 67: *Christopher Bell*

41, 117 (Bottom), 119 (Top): *Unknown, Courtesy of George and Joanne Frey*

54: *J. Llapitan, Courtesy of Marge Stovall, Silverwood Australian Shepherds*

65L *Unknown, Courtesy of Sharon Willis*

69, 182: *Linda Gray*

71, 135, 146: *Catherine Swain*

72: *Bonnie Daniels*

73: *Kohler Photography, Courtesy of Marge Stovall, Silverwood Australian Shepherds*

74 (Left), 148: *Pamela Levin*

74 (Right): *Vicky Mistretta*

75 (Left): *Robert Rogers, Courtesy of Kathy and Allan McCorkle*

75 (Right): *Linda Gray, Courtesy of Leslie Frank, Propwash Farm*

76: *Unknown, Courtesy of Dave & Bonnie Daniels*

78 (Right): *Callea Photo, Courtesy of Kathy and Allan McCorkle*

81: *Ron Bona Assoc., Courtesy of Sheila Polk*

Bibliography

Books

Bernstein, Susan. Editor. *Dog Digest*. DBI Books, Inc. Northfield, IL.

Bremness, Lesley. *The Complete Book of Herbs*. A Dorling Kindersley Book, Viking Studio Books. New York. 1988.

Bulanda, Susan. *Everything You Always Wanted to Know About Dogs*: 1992- 1993 Edition. Doral Publishing, Inc. Wilsonville, OR.

Campbell, William. *Behavior Problems in Dogs*. American Veterinary Publications, Inc. Goleta, CA. 1992.

Caplan, Linda and Clothier, Suzanne. *Agility Training Workbook*. Flying Dog Press. Frenchtown, NJ. 1989.

Green, Martin. *The Home Pet Vet Guide*. Ballantine Books. New York. 1980.

Grun, Bernard. *The Timetables of History: A Horizontal Linkage of People and Events*. A Touchstone Book, Simon and Schuster, New York, 1979.

Hart, Benjamin, DVM and Hart, Lynette. *The Perfect Puppy*. W. H. Freeman and Co. New York. 1988.

Hartnagle (Taylor), Jeanne Joy. *All About Aussies*. Alpine Publications, Inc. Loveland, CO. 1985.

Milon, Ellie. *201 Ways to Enjoy Your Dog*. Alpine Publications, Inc. Loveland, CO. 1990.

Pryor, Karen. *How to Teach Your Dog to Play Frisbee*. Simon and Schuster. New York. 1985.

Reader's Digest Association, Inc. *The Illustrated Encyclopedic Dictionary*. New York, 1987.

Rose, Tom and Patterson, Gary. *Training the Competitive Working Dog*. Giblaut Publishing Co. Englewood, CO. 1985.

Schwartz, Charlotte. *The Howell Book of Puppy Raising*. Howell Book House. New York. 1987.

Volhard, Jack and Bartlett, Melissa. *What all Good Dogs Should Know*. Howell Book House. New York. 1991.

Wilcox, Bonnie, DVM and Walkowicz, Chris. *Old Dogs, Old Friends*. Howell Book House. New York. 1991.

Magazine Articles, Booklets and Pamphlets

Aiello, Susan, DVM. *Vaccinations Are Important*. Dog Fancy. April 1988.

Akers-Hanson, Maryann. *The Making of a Show Dog*. Dog Fancy. Feb 1988.

Anderson, Moira. *Gastric Torsion*. Dog Fancy. Jan 1986.

Arden, Darlene. *Dr Gail Smith Forges New Frontiers in Hip Dysplasia*. Dog World. Dec 1990.

American Kennel Club. *Obedience Regulations. Guidelines for Dog Show Judges. Guidelines of Obedience Judges. Rules Applying to Registration and Dog Shows.*

Australian Shepherd Club of America. *Facts You Should Know Before Breeding Australian Shepherds,* flyer. *What is Hip Dysplasia*, flyer. *Basic Body Colors of the Australian Shepherd*, flyer. *Yearbook: 1957-1977 "Twenty Years of Progress."* *Stockdog Rules and Regulations. Show Rules and Regulations. Obedience Rules and Regulations.*

Ball, Sherry. *Judging the Australian Shepherd* AKC Purebred Dog Gazette, January 1993.

Begun, Ann. *Retinal Dysplasia*. AKC Purebred Dogs Gazette. Jan 1992.

Benjamin, Carol Lea. *Dog Trainer's Diary: Pet Evaluation Testing*. AKC Purebred Dogs Gazette. Oct 1991.

Brooks, Jeanne Freeman. *Call of the Wild*. San Diego Union-Tribune. Feb 6, 1994.

Busko, Susan. *A Journey of the Heart*. Aussie Times. July-Aug 1991.

California Veterinary Medical Association. *Guide to Pet Emergencies*.

Campbell, Roberta. *A Short Summary of the AKC Herding Program*. Off-Lead. March 1991.

Cargill, John, MA, MBA, MS. *What Should "Champion" Mean?* Dog World. Feb 1993. Genetic *Screening - Essential!* AKC Purebred Dogs Gazette. Jan 1991.

Carriera, Joanne. *Getting Started in Herding*. AKC Purebred Dogs Gazette. August 1992.

Chevreherd Australian Shepherds. *Building on a Solid Foundation.* Advertisement, Aussie Times. Nov-Dec 1993.

Coffin, C. A. *Genetic Nightmares.* Aussie Times. Date unknown.

David, Herm, PhD. *AKC Newswatch.* Dog World. July 1991.

Donoghue, Susan, VDM. *Nutrition: Vitamin and Mineral Supplements.* AKC Purebred Dogs Gazette. Oct 1993.

Dunbar, Ian, PhD, MRCVS. *Behavior: Puppy Aptitude Testing.* AKC Purebred Dogs Gazette. Feb 1989.

Fraser, Jacqueline. *Getting Started: Class Discussio*n. AKC Purebred Dogs Gazette. March 1989.

Hartnagle, Ernest. *The Spider Web: A Visual Representation of the line of descent in the Australian Shepherd.*

Herbel, Lori. *AKC Herding: Better Than Ever.* AKC Purebred Dogs Gazette. November 1991.

Hoffman, Patricia Bennett. *Bloat: Seeking Answers.* AKC Purebred Dogs Gazette. April 1989.

Johnson, Andy. *Australian Shepherd: Total Dog.* Dog World, March 1984

Keller, G. DVM, MS; D. Vogt, PhD; E. A. Corley, DVM, PhD; G. Padgett, DVM; and M. Ellersieck, PhD. *Progress in the Control of Hip Dysplasia.* AKC Purebred Dogs Gazette. Nov 1991.

Little, Maryland. *Happy Herding Handbook.*

Lofthouse, Kathryn. *The English Shepherd Today* UKC Bloodlines, May - June 1992

Mackenzie, Dana. *The Future of the Working Australian Shepherd.* Ranch Dog Trainer. Oct- November 1993

Milne, Edward L. *The Australian Shepherd Controversy.* Dog Watch. Oct 4, 1991.

Myers, Sarah, PhD. *Breeders Forum: Placing Puppies in the '90s.* AKC Purebred Dogs Gazette.

Reidarson, Thomas H., DVM. *Bloat.* Dog Fancy. June 1990.

Riddle, Lenora. *Fanciers Forum: Australian Shepherd Wrangle*; Splinter Group Joins AKC Dog Fancy, September 1991

Rhodes, Elsie. *The All American Australian Shepherd.* AKC Purebred Dogs Gazette. Oct 1991.

Sammon, Edy. *It's Show Time*! Dog Fancy. Oct 1986.

Sawyer, Jennifer. *Two Young Ladies, A Young Man and an Aussie.* Aussie Times, July-Aug 1991.

Sharp, C. A. *Collie Eye Anomaly: What it Means to the Aussie Breeder.* Aussie Times, Jan-Feb 1992.

Sorenson, Kim. *Progressive Retinal Atrophy Spreads Through Dogdom.* Dog World. May 1990.

Spencer, James B. *Launching AKC's Herding Trials.* AKC Purebred Dogs Gazette. July 1990. *A Look at AKC's Herding test and Trials.* Gazette. October 1989.

Purebred World: What Does "Ch" Really Mean? Dog Fancy. March 1988.

Finding a Four-legged Ranch Hand. Dog Fancy. March 1987.

Strand, Patti. *Overpopulation: Do Statistics Tell the Whole Story?* AKC Purebred Dogs Gazette. March 1993.

Strom, Judith. *Working Ranch Dogs.* AKC Purebred Dogs Gazette. December 1990.

Swift, W. Bradford, DVM. *Don't Get Ticked!* Dog Fancy. Aug 1991.

Walkowicz, Chris. *Breeders Forum: To Neuter or Not to Neuter.* AKC Purebred Dogs Gazette. January 1989.

Breeders Forum: Why OFA, CERF, VWD? AKC Purebred Dogs Gazette.

Wilcox, Bonnie, DVM. *Internal Parasites.* Dog Fancy. July 1990.

Index

There is nothing like cooling off in a ditch full of water.